# For Every Child, An Equal Chance

The History, People, and Rosenwald Schools of The West Tennessee Educational Congress in Memphis and Rural Shelby County

1902-1966

Wynn E. Earle, Jr.

Published by Beacon Light Stories LLC
Memphis, Tennessee


For additional information, contact Beacon Light Stories at:
Email: wynn.earle@beaconlightstories.com


Visit us online at http://www.beaconlightstories.com.

*For my wife, Clara*

My love, my confidante, my air

# CONTENTS

# Acknowledgments

I am deeply grateful to the people who assisted me with preparing this book. I am forever grateful to every living person, family member, and relative of the deceased educators upon whom I called and depended for information, documents, and photographs that contributed to its accuracy and completeness.

While archive collections are credited, I owe a special thanks to George Whitworth, whose collection contained wonderful stories, documents, and photographs used in this book. I also owe a special thanks to Raka Nandi of the Memphis Museum of Science and History for including me in conversations to save the old President's Island School. This opportunity put me in contact with retired AP History teacher Mark Scott, whose work to save the President's Island School is informative and inspiring. In addition, thank you to the many people, including Rev. Dr. Clennon Saulsberry, Sr., Florenstine S. Woods, and Julia Earle Williamson, for access to their private collections. I am also grateful to Dr. Ticada Currie, Mrs. Kacy Barber, and Mr. Arthur Humphrey for giving me valuable feedback on the flow of this book as it neared completion.

Finally, a special thank you to Dollie Pugh Hall, Gladys Pugh Lewis, Willie Dean Sain and Florence Quinn-Davis for sharing their stories of school life in the 1930s, 1940s, and 1950s. Your heartfelt reflections on your school days have, hopefully, helped me craft a story as rich as your memories.

# Special Contributor

## MR. JOHN E. STRONG, JR.

Mr. John E. Strong, Jr. made essential contributions to the development and flow of this book. A life-long resident of Northern Shelby County, he and his family's influence on education in Shelby County for over a century is well documented. He is a 1948 graduate of Barret's Chapel High School, a 1952 graduate of Lane College, and a 1962 graduate of Tennessee A & I State University. During a February 2023 recording of a Beacon Light Stories Podcast episode, Mr. Strong shared vivid stories of his youth as a student at Anthony Chapel School and Barret's Chapel High School and his time as a teacher and principal at Brunswick Jr. High, Geeter High, Eads Jr. High, Weaver Elementary, Capleville High, and Woodstock High School. His stories were invaluable to this book's growth because not many people can share first-hand accounts of what schools in Northern Shelby County were like in the 1930s and 1940s. The detail and clarity of his shared stories inspired the author to share as many stories, photographs, and facts about schools in Memphis and rural Shelby County as possible.

Most importantly, Mr. Strong inspired the author to think deeply about the legacy that he is leaving. Strong is a dedicated Alpha Phi Alpha Fraternity, Inc. brother who never shies away from opportunities to help his community. Mr. Strong and the author are brothers in Alpha, and he considers Mr. Strong a trusted friend who inspires him to be a better husband, educator, leader, and historian.

# Introduction

*4* One generation commends your works to
another; they tell of your mighty acts. *5* They
speak of the glorious splendor of your
majesty – and I will meditate on your
wonderful works. *6* They tell of the power of
your awesome works – and I will proclaim
your great deeds.

*(Psalm 145:4-6)*

I was fortunate to have either attended or had a relationship with individuals who attend some of the schools of the West Tennessee Educational Congress (WTEC). Some of my fondest memories of school occurred at Shannon Elementary in North Memphis. The school, led by Douglass High School (c/o 1955) and Tennessee A & I State College (c/o 1959) graduate Mr. Halloe Robinson, was filled with veteran teachers who stressed the importance of education. The first books that I remember checking out at the school's library were written by Augusta Stevenson: Abe Lincoln, Frontier Boy, and Booker T. Washington Ambitious Boy. I checked them out so frequently that I can remember the tales of young Abe Lincoln reading by candlelight close to the fireplace in his family's cabin and how young Booker T. Washington helped to feed the pigs and chickens, but most of all, he wanted to go to school. During those early years, Mr. Robinson's nurturing environment at Shannon Elementary sparked my love of history and schools.

I loved school. As a high school student, I had the privilege to learn the subtleties of choral music from Hamilton High School (c/o 1955) and Fisk University (c/o 1959) graduate Dr. Lulah M. Hedgeman. As I grew older, my late grandmother, Fannie T. Earle, shared stories of attending Barret's Chapel High School, where Tennessee A & I graduate (c/o 1926) Mr. Guy Hoffman was a leader of the school and the surrounding community. When I married, my grandmother realized that she was a high school classmate of the uncle and aunts of my wife: Mr. Aubrey C. Pugh, Mrs. Ruth Pugh Singleton, and Mrs. Gladys Pugh Lewis. During Thanksgiving Dinners, I would listen to them talk about how they lived with family near the school during the week and returned home on the weekends. They did this because there was not a public high school for African American children in Mason, TN. My mother-in-law, Dollie Pugh Hall, who graduated from Gailor Industrial High School in Mason, TN, often reflects on how she didn't have to leave home to attend Barret's Chapel because Gailor Industrial School, which was once Gailor Episcopal School, was now a free, public high school. These stories inspired me to learn more about these schools and schools like them. While researching the history of schools in rural Shelby County, I learned more about the Colored Teacher Associations (CTAs) across Tennessee.

The Colored Teachers Associations were crucial in developing African American education, particularly after the Civil War. Established in 1861, these organizations became vital platforms for African American educators to advocate for improved education for Black children, foster professional development, and address broader socio-political issues within the Black community. They helped to shape both educational policy and pedagogical practices at a time when African Americans faced significant racial discrimination and segregation in the educational system.

The first CTA, founded in Ohio in 1861, responded to the lack of professional networks for African American teachers and the dire educational circumstances of African American students. Over the next few decades, CTAs grew, particularly in southern states, where Black educators and parents faced numerous challenges due to racial segregation and underfunding of schools for African American children. In 1903, the CTAs formed a national body known as the National Association of Negro Teachers, which was renamed the National Association of Teachers in Colored Schools (NATCS) in 1907 and ultimately became the American Teachers Association (ATA) in 1937. The WTEC, founded in 1902, was one of the earliest CTAs founded in Tennessee.

The purpose of the WTEC was to 1) Raise the standard of education, 2) Improve the methods of instruction, 3) Promote a deeper interest in the cause of education, 4) and 5) Build a favorable sentiment on behalf of colored schools. The WTEC provided space for African American teachers to exchange ideas and best practices, which was not readily available elsewhere due to the segregated nature of professional organizations. These groups held regular meetings and published journals to document their activities, share educational research, and provide updates on critical issues affecting African American communities.

The WTEC was deeply connected to the historically Black colleges and universities (HBCUs), Black churches, and social organizations in West Tennessee, including Greek-letter fraternities and sororities. Many of the members of these associations were also involved in the more significant Black civic and social movements of the time. The organizations collaborated closely with the Colored Parent-Teacher Associations to further their goals of improving the educational experience for African American children. In the WTEC, the presidents and faculties of Lane College, LeMoyne College, and Tennessee State University provided leadership to WTEC and were home to the organization's annual conferences. The WTEC was instrumental in organizing school competitions, educational conferences, and advocacy campaigns. It also served as an essential network for African American educators to advance their careers and improve the quality of teaching and learning in their communities.

The WTEC published journals monthly starting in 1928. These journals served several purposes: they documented the organization's activities, recorded the work of its leadership, shared instructional ideals, and provided a forum for discussions on issues related to Black education. These publications were vital tools for maintaining communication between members, advocating for change, and documenting the successes of Black educators and schools.

The post-Brown v. Board of Education era significantly changed advocating for education in African American communities. Following the 1954 Supreme Court ruling that declared racial segregation in public schools unconstitutional, CTAs in northern and southern states began to merge with their white counterparts in state-level education associations. In 1964, the National Education Association (NEA) passed a resolution requiring state affiliates to remove racial membership restrictions and develop integration plans. By the early 1970s, most southern CTAs merged with the white teacher associations, marking the end of the segregated educational organizations that had been essential to African American educators for over a century. The WTEC merged with the TEA in 1966.

The WTEC's legacy is profound. Not only did it provide a professional space for African American educators, but they were also key players in the fight for educational equity in West Tennessee. They laid the groundwork for integrating African American teachers into mainstream educational systems and helped shape policies designed to improve the educational experiences of African American students. The WTEC's influence can still be felt in the ongoing work of modern educators throughout West Tennessee.

The legacy of the WTEC also reminds us of the resilience and resourcefulness of Black educators who, in the face of systemic racism, created networks of support that were essential to personal and community development. The WTEC helped ensure that African American educators were not only advocates for their students but also critical voices in shaping the future of education across the country.

This book is mostly about educators in Memphis and rural Shelby County who made it possible for children to learn and grow at difficult times. It is my "Thank You" to each educator highlighted in this book. Most of the individuals in this book now hold the title of "ancestor," so I cannot physically thank them for their great deeds, but as an author, I can ensure that stories of their works live on for new generations to appreciate and learn from.

Finally, I hope this book will give Memphians, non-Memphians, Shelby County Residents, and non-Shelby County Residents, young and old, a deeper appreciation of why our schools, flaws, and all. Simply put, this book is my view of the evolution of public education for African Americans in Memphis and rural Shelby County that fights *For Every Child* to have *An Equal Chance*.

# Chapter One

# The History of The West Tennessee Educational Congress

The West Tennessee Educational Congress (WTEC) was founded in 1902 in Martin, Tennessee. It was one of the three grand divisions of Tennessee Negro Education Association (TNEC) which was founded on July 23, 1923. The other associations within the TNEC were the East Tennessee Teachers Association and the Middle Tennessee Teachers Association. Until 1938, the TNEC was named the Tennessee State Association of Teachers in Colored Schools. According to records, the idea to start an association for the African American teachers, principals, and supervisors in West Tennessee was credited to these men and women educators: John William Johnson (Weakley County), William Robert Jarrett (Obion County), Rev. Albert J. Collins (Madison County), Marshall Lee Morrison, Sr. (Dyer County), William Henry Fort, Sr. (Weakley County), Austin Raymond Merry (Madison County), Thomas Marion Stigall (Gibson County), Joseph F. Booker (Gibson County), Dr. James Albert. Bray (Lane College), Dr. James Franklin Lane (Lane College), Dr. Simon William Broome, Sr. (Fayette County), William Parker Ware (Fayette County), Eugene Alston (Tipton County), John Robert Gloster (Shelby County), W.G. Webster (Tipton County), Charles Julius Neal, Sr. (Shelby County), George Frederick Porter (Madison County), Mrs. Ollie Stigall (Gibson County), Mrs. Jennie Booker (Gibson County), and Mrs. Florence Nelson (Lauderdale County). John William Johnson, who served as the first president of the WTEC from 1902-1909, stated during the WTEC's fiftieth-anniversary conference in 1952, "We didn't know at that time that we had started anything that would grow into what I see here today."

At the time of the WTEC's founding, schools that served African American children lacked the basic accommodations that we see in schools today. Many schools were wood frame structures in the larger cities and the smaller rural towns. Often, churches doubled as schools, with the occasional school housed in a community masonic lodge. Additionally, the subjects and methods to teach those subjects varied from school to school and county to county. A program from an early WTEC Annual Conference states that "The purpose of the West Tennessee Educational Congress shall be to raise the standard of education, to improve the methods of instruction, to promote a deeper interest in the cause of education, and to build a favorable sentiment in behalf of colored schools."

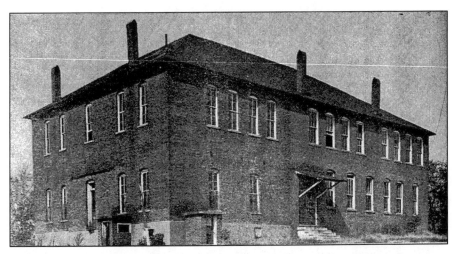

The establishment of the WTEC gave African American teachers, principals, and supervisors in West Tennessee the platform to share ideas and concerns with colleagues across the region. These educational leaders now had an organized way of exchanging ideas that could improve instruction through new techniques and methods. Most importantly, these discussions could be held freely and openly. During those early years, African American schools were appointed supervisors for elementary and industrial instruction and teachers for vocational, agriculture, and home economics. Pictured above is the Martin Colored High School in Martin, Tennessee, the site of the founding of the WTEC in 1902, where John William Johnson, the first president of the WTEC, was the principal. Pictured below is the building that replaced the old building above. It was renamed the Weakley County Training School. (Courtesy of the Tennessee State University Special Collection)

The years following the founding of the WTEC saw several challenges and triumphs for the African American Schools in the region. Across the region, schools struggled to upgrade their buildings. Many schools in rural Shelby County were established or improved with the support of the Rosenwald Fund. The Rosenwald Fund was a partnership between philanthropist and co-owner of Sears, Roebuck, and Co., Julius Rosenwald, and founding principal of the Tuskegee Institute, Booker T. Washington, to partner with African American communities across the rural South to build schools. Between 1917 and 1930, sixty Rosenwald Schools were built in Shelby County. During the same period, over 20 Rosenwald Schools were built in Fayette County and at least 10 schools were constructed in Tipton County. Across the South, the Rosenwald Fund built nearly 5,000 schools between 1912 and 1937.

Two other funds also supported building schools and improving teaching in African American Schools in West Tennessee: The Slater Fund and the Jeanes Fund. The Slater Fund was an endowment established by American philanthropist John Fox Slater in 1882 to educate African Americans in the South. The Jeanes Fund was named after American philanthropist Anna T. Jeanes whose foundation helped support the education of African Americans in rural communities in the South beginning in 1908. Pictured above is a souvenir button from the Tennessee Negro Education Association Conference on the campus of Tennessee A & I University in 1949. (Courtesy of a private collection)

Pictured above is a group of WTEC delegates at the TNEA Convention led by WTEC President Cornell Wells, principal of E.A. Harrold School in Millington, TN, in 1963. Below is the Shelby County Training School choir performing at the 1953 TNEA Convention. (Courtesy of the Tennessee State University Special Collection)

A highlight of the WTEC was the annual conferences that were held in locations around the region. In the early days of the WTEC, the conference would be held in a county, with meetings and training being held at the largest school. Held in October or November, schools across the region were usually closed so teachers and administrators could attend the conference. Some locations of the earliest WTEC conferences were Dyersburg, Dresden, Memphis, and Fulton, KY. As their numbers grew, the annual conferences were held on the campus of Lange College in Jackson, TN, or Tennessee A & I University in Nashville. In addition to Lane College Presidents Dr. James F. Lane and Dr. James A. Bray, Tennessee A & I President Dr. Walter S. Davis, and Professors Dr. Merl R. Eppse and Dr. George W. Gore, Jr were instrumental in the growth of the WTEC. Pictured above is Elementary Education Chairwoman E.B. Seets, speaking to conference Attendees in 1953. Below is a meeting of the history and social studies committee members during the 1953 Convention. (Courtesy of the Tennessee State University Special Collection)

Robert E. Clay, left, was instrumental in the growth of Rosenwald Schools in Tennessee. Professor Clay, or "Daddy" Clay, was appointed the Rosenwald School Agent in 1917 by the special act of the Tennessee Legislature. Between 1917 and 1937, Professor Clay helped establish over 500 hundred Rosenwald Schools in rural, county, and city communities across Tennessee. In 1937, he was appointed the developer of Negro Education for the Tennessee State Department of Education. He served in this capacity until his retirement in 1955. An associate of Dr. Booker T. Washington, Clay worked with Washington in the early years of the National Negro Business League of America. A 1932 graduate of Tennessee A & I University, the R. E. Clay Education Building on the campus of Tennessee State University is named in his honor. (Courtesy of the Tennessee State University Special Collection)

Dr. George W. Gore, Sr., left, was an early supporter of the West Tennessee Educational Congress. A Nashville native, he earned his A.B. degree from DePauw University in 1923, a Master of Education degree from Harvard University in 1928, and a Ph.D. from Columbia University in 1939. From 1923 to 1950, Gore served as the executive secretary of the Tennessee Negro Education Association (TNEA). During the same period, he was a professor of English and Journalism at Tennessee A & I. In 1950, Gore was named the president of Florida A&M University, where he served until 1968. In addition to serving as the TNEA secretary during the Great Depression and WWII, Dr. Gore was of the Association of Colleges from 1950 to 1951 and the American Teachers Association from 1949 to 1951. He was a member of Alpha Phi Alpha Fraternity, Inc. (Courtesy of the Tennessee State University Special Collection)

The Jeanes Supervisors in Shelby County were instrumental to the growth of the WTEC. Jeanes Supervisors, who got their name from Philadelphia philanthropist Anne T. Jeanes, were women who worked to improve the conditions of the schools and the surrounding communities. These women, sometimes called Jeanes Teachers or Jeanes Workers, ensured that teachers were trained, parents were involved in the life of their community's school, and children's health and living conditions improved wherever they lived. Each of these supervisors experienced success as teachers and principals before being appointed by the Memphis and Shelby County superintendent to be the Jeanes Supervisor.

Mrs. Lucille Hansborough Brewer was named supervisor of Negro Schools in Memphis City Schools in 1951. Her primary focus was supervising the quality of instruction in the city's elementary schools. A 1918 graduate of Kortrecht High School, she began her career in Memphis City Schools in 1920. Before becoming supervisor, she served as principal of Klondike Elementary from 1946 to 1951. Before Klondike, she taught at Porter Jr. High School. Mrs. Brewer earned a Bachelor of Arts Degree from LeMoyne College. (Courtesy of a private collection)

Mrs. Elizabeth N. Townsend was named supervisor of the Negro Schools of Shelby County in 1951. Before being named supervisor, Mrs. Townsend served as Capleville School's principal, which was located outside of the Memphis City limits. Mrs. Townsend earned a Bachelor of Science degree from LeMoyne College in 1939, and a Master of Science in Educational Supervision in 1952. (Courtesy of the Tennessee State University Special Collection)

Jim Ella Cotton was appointed a supervisor of the Negro School in Memphis City Schools in 1958. Before her appointment, she served as the principal of Klondike School from 1952 to 1958. Miss Cotton began her teaching career in Memphis in 1916. She taught at LaRose, Greenwood, and Booker T. Washington High School. In 1933, she earned a bachelor's degree from LeMoyne College and a master's degree from Columbia University years later. Miss Cotton was a member of Sigma Gamma Rho Sorority, Inc. (Courtesy of a private collection)

# WEST TENNESSEE EDUCATIONAL CONGRESS PRESIDENTS

John William Johnson was the first president of the West Tennessee Educational Congress (WTEC). He was president for the first seven years of the WTEC's existence, 1902-1909. Professor Johnson was an 1889 graduate of Roger Williams University in Nashville, Tennessee. Professor Johnson earned a master's degree from Brown University. Johnson taught and served as a principal in Weakley County, Tennessee, during this time. He was named Roger Williams University's first African American president in 1909. When the university closed, he taught at Morehead State University in Atlanta, Georgia, until his retirement. (Courtesy of the Tennessee State University Special Collection)

Austin Raymond Merry served as the second president of the WTEC from 1909 to 1910. Professor Raymond earned a Bachelor of Arts degree and a master's degree from Fisk University. After graduating, he settled in Jackson, Tennessee, and became the first African American to earn a college degree in Jackson. Merry established Jackson's first school for African Americans in the mid-1870s and the city's first chapter of the NAACP. The school was renamed Merry High School after he died in 1921. Jackson Central–Merry High School takes its name partly after Professor Merry. (Courtesy of the Tennessee State University Special Collection)

Edward Lincoln Honesty served as the third president of the WTEC from 1911 to 1912. A graduate of Mechanicsburg High School and Oberlin College in Ohio, Professor Honesty taught and was principal for over 50 years. In 1892, he was appointed the assistant principal of Kortrecht High School, G.P. Hamilton. Later, he became the principal of Kortrecht Grammar School. Before retiring, he served as the principal of Grant School in Memphis. (Courtesy of a private collection)

** 4th President, John R. Gloster, of Brownsville, TN, is not pictured. He served from 1913 to 1914. He was an 1880 LeMoyne Normal School graduate and served as the Dunbar (Haywood County Training School) principal from 1886 to 1915. His son, Dr. Hugh Morris Gloster, taught at LeMoyne College and served as the president of Morehouse College from 1967-1987. **

Marshall Lee Morrison, Sr. of Dyersburg, Tennessee, served as the fifth president from 1914 to 1915. Professor Morrison graduated from Lane College in Jackson and the University of West Tennessee in Memphis. He began teaching in 1892 and was named principal of Bruce High School in Dyersburg in 1911. He remained there until his retirement in 1946. (Courtesy of Lane College Collection)

George Frederick Porter was the WTEC's sixth president from 1915 to 1916. A graduate of Lane College, Professor Porter also served Lane College as the normal school principal, teacher, and treasurer between 1906 and 1928 before being elected treasurer for the CME Church. (Courtesy of Lane College Collection)

Lawyer E. Brown was the seventh president of the WTEC. He served from 1916 to 1917. Professor Brown, a graduate of LeMoyne College in Memphis, TN, and Fisk University in Nashville, TN, served as the dean of Black Principals in Memphis. He was appointed principal of the Porter School in Memphis, TN in 1920. He would serve as the Porter's principal for 25 years. (Courtesy of the Tennessee State University Special Collection)

William Robert Jarret served as the eighth president of the WTEC from 1917 to 1921. Professor Jarret taught and was a principal in West Tennessee for 57 years. His wife, Annie Jarret, taught in elementary schools in West Tennessee for over 50 years. Their son, Dr. Thomas Dunbar Jarrett, served as the seventh president of Atlanta University from 1968 to 1977. (Courtesy of the Tennessee State University Special Collection)

** 9th and 10th WTEC Presidents Reverend Albert J. Collins of Jackson, TN, a graduate of Roger Williams University in Nashville, and Reverend Joseph James Bills of Obion County are not pictured. **

Pictured right is the eleventh president, Thomas J. Johnson, who served from 1924-1930. Professor Johnson was a graduate of Alcorn A&M College in Mississippi. In 1912, he established the Shelby County Training School at Woodstock, TN. Johnson was the principal from 1912 to 1927 before becoming the principal of Klondike Elementary School in Memphis, TN. He would remain the principal of Klondike until his retirement in 1949. (Courtesy of the Tennessee State University Special Collection)

Green Polonius "G.P." Hamilton was the twelfth West Tennessee Educational Congress president from 1930 to 1931. He attended LeMoyne Normal Institute in Memphis, TN, Rust College in Holly Springs, MS, and Columbia University in New York. He served as the principal of Kortrecht High School (renamed Booker T. Washington High School in 1926) in Memphis, TN, from 1892 until he died in 1932. (Courtesy of the Tennessee State University Special Collection)

Andrew Jackson "A.J." Payne, the thirteenth president of the WTEC, served from 1931 to 1932. Professor Payne attended Lane College in Jackson, TN, Atlanta University, and the University of Chicago. He served as principal of Merry High School in Jackson, Tennessee, from 1921 to 1948. Before serving as Merry High School's principal, Payne was a coach and math teacher in Gibson and Madison Counties in Tennessee. (Courtesy of the Tennessee State University Special Collection)

Pictured left is the fourteenth WTEC president, Dr. Festus Eugene "F.E." Jefferies. Dr. Jefferies served as the WTEC president from 1932 to 1933. He was the principal of the Dunbar School (renamed the Haywood County Training School in 1922) from 1916 to 1936. Because of the school's focus, he was known as the "Agriculture Man". He was named the county's first African American Agricultural Extension Agent in 1936. (Courtesy of the Tennessee State University Special Collection)

Lucie E. Campbell-Williams served as the West Tennessee Educational Congress president from 1933-1934. Mrs. Campbell-Williams was the first woman to hold the position of WTEC President. Mrs. Campbell-Williams, a graduate of Rust College in Holly Springs, MS, Tennessee A&I University in Nashville, TN, and Columbia University in New York, was a well-known music educator and song composer. She was an educator in Memphis, mainly at Booker T. Washington High School, for over 50 years. She retired in 1954. (Courtesy of a private collection)

James Luther Seets served as the sixteenth and twenty-first president of the WTEC. He served for three years, 1934 to 1936 and 1941 to 1942. He served as the first principal of the Carroll County Training School in McKenzie, Tennessee, beginning in 1920. The school was renamed Webb High School after John L. Webb in 1936. Professor Seets would serve as principal of Webb High School until his retirement in 1957. Professor Seets was a member of Kappa Alpha Psi Fraternity, Inc. (Courtesy of a private collection)

Lorenzo Miller, pictured left, was the seventeenth president of the WTEC from 1937 to 1938. He earned a Bachelor of Science in 1927 and a Master of Science in 1951 from Tennessee A & I State College in Nashville, Tennessee. Professor Miller served as the principal of the Bolivar Industrial School in Bolivar, TN, for 42 years. Alongside his wife, Frances, who served as the school's home economics teacher, Professor Miller served the school faithfully until his retirement in 1968. (Courtesy of the Tennessee State University Special Collection)

George W. Brooks was the eighteenth president of the West Tennessee Educational Congress from 1938 to 1939. During his time in public education, Professor Brooks was the principal of Frazier High School in Covington and Burt High School in Clarksville, TN, before retiring in 1968. In addition to his service to WTEC, he served as the president of the Tennessee Negro Education Association (TNEA). Professor Brooks was a member of Alpha Phi Alpha Fraternity, Inc. (Courtesy of the Tennessee State University Special Collection)

The nineteenth president of the West Tennessee Educational Congress was Roy B. Bond. He served as president from 1939 to 1940. Professor Bond was a graduate of Lane College in Jackson, TN. He was named the principal of Haywood County Training School (renamed Carver High School in 1950) in 1936 when the fourteenth president of the WTEC, F.E. Jeffries, left to become the county's agricultural extension agent. Professor Bond served as principal of Carver High until the school's closure in 1970. (Courtesy of the Tennessee State University Special Collection)

Dr. Claude C. Bond was the twentieth president of the West Tennessee Educational Congress, serving from 1940 to 1941. He graduated from Lane College, Fisk University, and George Peabody College in Nashville, Tennessee. He taught in Henderson County for 23 years, 21 of which were as principal of Montgomery High School. He later served as principal of Howard High School in Chattanooga. (Courtesy of the Tennessee State University Special Collection)

Floyd Campbell, pictured left, was the twenty-second president of the WTEC. Professor Campbell served as president from 1943 to 1944. He graduated from Morehouse College in Atlanta and earned a master's degree from Atlanta University. Campbell served as a teacher at Manassas High School in Memphis before being appointed the principal of Kortrecht Intermediate, Porter Jr. High, and, finally, Melrose High School. His career spanned 43 years, and he was the principal of Melrose High for twenty years, from 1949 to 1969. Professor Campbell was a member of Kappa Alpha Psi Fraternity, Inc. (Courtesy of a private collection)

Pictured left is the twenty-third West Tennessee Educational Congress president, Dr. Hollis F. Price. Dr. Price was president from 1945 to 1946 and was the first African American President of LeMoyne College in Memphis. He graduated from Amherst College and earned a master's degree from Columbia University. His presidency at LeMoyne College spanned from 1943 to 1970. Before his tenure at LeMoyne College, he served as a professor of economics at Tuskegee University for sixteen years. Dr. Price was a member of Alpha Phi Alpha Fraternity, Inc. (Courtesy of the Memphis Public Library & Information Center)

Richard H. Neville was the twenty-fourth president of the WTEC. From 1946 to 1947, Professor Neville graduated from the LeMoyne Normal Institute. He was an educator in Memphis, serving as a teacher at Carnes School before his appointment to principal of Greenwood School. After his time at Greenwood, Neville was appointed principal of Melrose High School and Klondike Elementary before his retirement. He also served as the president of the Tennessee State Association of Teachers in Colored Schools. (Courtesy of the Tennessee State University Special Collection)

Pictured left is Blair T. Hunt. He served as the twenty-fifth president of the WTEC from 1947-1948. Professor Hunt was the second-ever principal of Booker T. Washington High School in Memphis, serving as the principal for 24 years, from 1932 to 1956. He attended the LeMoyne Normal Institute, Tennessee A & I College, Harvard University, and Columbia University. He was also an Elder in the Disciples of Christ Church, serving as the first senior pastor of Mississippi Boulevard Christian Church in Memphis from 1921 to 1973. Rev. Hunt was a member of Alpha Phi Alpha Fraternity, Inc. (Courtesy of a private collection)

James Ashton Hayes was the twenty-sixth West Tennessee Educational Congress president, from 1949 to 1950. Hayes was a graduate of Lane College in Jackson, Tennessee. He began his career as a teacher in West Tennessee and Kentucky. For 23 years, he served as principal of Manassas High School in Memphis from 1929 to 1952. Professor Hayes retired in 1955 as principal of Lester Elementary School. (Courtesy of the Tennessee State University Special Collection)

William W. Mays, pictured left, was the twenty-seventh president of the West Tennessee Educational Congress. Professor Mays' tenure as president spanned one year, 1951 to 1952. During his time in public education, Professor Mays was the principal of Frazier High School in Covington, Tennessee, and Burt High School in Clarksville before retiring in 1968. In addition to his service to WTEC, he served as the president of the Tennessee Negro Education Association. (Courtesy of the Tennessee State University Special Collection)

Harry Mae Simons, the twenty-eighth president of the West Tennessee Educational Congress, served for two years, from 1952 to 1954. Principal Simons received her bachelor's degree from LeMoyne College in 1932 and a Master of Science in Education from Tennessee A & I State College in 1947. She retired in 1980 after thirty-six years as an educator in Memphis, including 33 years as the principal of Magnolia Elementary. She was a member of Sigma Gamma Rho Sorority, Inc. (Courtesy of the Tennessee State University Special Collection)

William E. Ledbetter, of Selmar, Tennessee, was the twenty-ninth president of the WTEC. He served as president from 1954 to 1956. Professor Ledbetter was a 1941 graduate of Lane College in Jackson, TN, and a 1956 graduate of Tennessee A&I State University. He was named the principal of McNairy County High School in 1940. (Courtesy of the Tennessee State University Special Collection)

Roy Jacob Roddy, left, was the thirtieth president of the WTEC. Professor Roddy served as president from 1956 to 1958. He earned a Bachelor of Science in 1946 and a Master of Science in 1960 from Tennessee A & I State University. Roddy began his career as a teacher at the Shelby County Training School (Woodstock High School) in 1920. He became the second principal in the school's history when T.J. Johnson left in 1928. He remained the principal until his retirement in 1966. (Courtesy of the Tennessee State University Special Collection)

Pictured left is Arthur Lee Robinson, the thirty-first West Tennessee Educational Congress president. Professor Robinson's tenure as president spanned four years, from 1958 to 1962. In 1942, he earned a Bachelor of Science degree from Tennessee A&I State College and a Master of Science degree in Agricultural Education in 1951, also from Tennessee A&I. During his time in public education, Professor Robinson served as a teacher and the principal of Montgomery High School in Lexington, TN from 1937 to 1974. (Courtesy of the Tennessee State University Special Collection)

Cornell Lawrence Wells, the thirty-second president of the WTEC, earned a Bachelor of Science degree from LeMoyne College in 1950 and a Master of Science degree in Education Administration in 1958 from Tennessee A & I State University. He served as the president of the WTEC from 1962 to 1963. Wells served as a teacher and administrator in Memphis for forty-plus years, from 1932 to 1977. He first taught at the Hamner-Taylor School at age 18 and was named principal of the Spring Hill School in 1933 at the age of 19. He served as the principal of E.A. Harrold from 1938-1968 before becoming an assistant superintendent in 1970, becoming the first African American promoted to that role in Memphis City Schools history in 1970. (Courtesy of the Tennessee State University Special Collection)

Torris Jacob "T.J." Toney was the thirty-third president of the West Tennessee Educational Congress. Professor Toney's tenure as president spanned from 1964 to 1965. He graduated from LeMoyne College, where he received a bachelor's degree in education, and in 1960, he earned a master's degree from Tuskegee Institute. A member of Alpha Phi Alpha Fraternity, Inc., Toney served as a teacher at Woodstock School in Millington, TN, assistant principal at Geeter High School, and principal at Weaver Elementary before being named principal at Geeter High School in 1960. He retired from Memphis City Schools in 1972. (Courtesy of Collection of Rev. Dr. Clennon Saulsberry, Sr.)

# Chapter Two

# Schools in Southwest Shelby County (Whitehaven, South Memphis and Orange Mound)

## GEETER HIGH SCHOOL (ROSENWALD)

Geeter School is one of the earliest schools for African Americans in Shelby County. The exact date of the opening of the first Geeter School is unknown, but the Commercial Appeal Newspaper first mentioned the Geeter School in 1906. That year, Lucy Jane Jay was the school's teacher. In 1909, Callie Mathis was the school's teacher, and Estelle Campbell was the assistant at Geeter School. Louise Polk and Annie Perkins were Geeter's teachers in 1919. In 1921, Dr. Joseph W. Falls was appointed the principal of Geeter. At the time, Geeter was a grammar school with three teachers, including his wife, Montee Norman Falls. The first school was a wooden frame four-room structure. Pictured above is the school in the 1920s. Pictured in the background is the principal's home. (Courtesy of a private collection)

Geeter School began to grow quickly under Dr. Fall's leadership. The school set forth the following objective: To develop and maintain Christian Character, Intellectual Attainment, Physical Health, Well-Adjusted Personality, Vocational Efficiency, and Inspiration for Service. By 1924, Geeter participated in the city-wide fairs where students showcased home and farm exhibits, proof of the training they received. Students submitted entries of handmade garments and canned fruits and vegetables. In the early 1930s, Geeter began offering night classes focusing on vocational and academic skills such as shoemaking and literacy. Under the leadership of Dr. Falls, a junior high was added in 1925, and a senior high program was added by Shelby County in 1930. In 1931, Geeter's first graduating class received their high school diplomas. During the flood of 1937, displaced African American citizens took shelter at the school. Pictured is the new elementary building that was completed in 1952. It was a 12-room structure with a gymnasium, science laboratory, and a remodeled home economics building. (Courtesy of the Tennessee State University Special Collection)

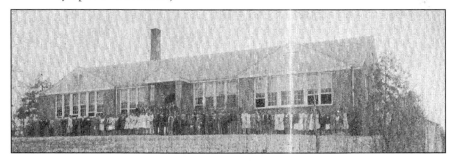

Professor Joseph W. Falls was more than just the principal of Geeter High School. Born in Somerville, TN, Falls attended several schools, including LeMoyne Institute, Tennessee A&I State College, Rust College, and Alabama A&M University. Later, he received an honorary doctoral degree from Monrovia College in Liberia, West Africa. When he was appointed principal in 1921 at 26, Geeter was a small wood frame school with three teachers. (Courtesy of Collection of Rev. Dr. Clennon Saulsberry, Sr.)

By 1955, the school had 51 teachers and 1500 students from all over Shelby County and Mississippi. Falls helped build a six-room addition and auditorium to accommodate the school's growth. He even laid the bricks for this first brick building on campus. Dr. Falls also purchased the first school bus for the school and served as the driver for the first two years. Daily, he picked up students from the Capleville, Boxtown, Brooks Avenue, Hamner-Taylor, and Weaver Communities. Pictured below is the 15-room addition that was completed in 1956. (Courtesy of the Tennessee State University Special Collection)

As the school grew, vocational training in cooking, sewing, laundry, brick masonry, woodwork, blacksmith, auto mechanics, and music were available to students. As time progressed, instruction in the literary arts, math, and sciences became the school's primary focus. Professor Falls ensured his students were exposed to opportunities that would help them become well-rounded citizens. An ordained minister, Dr. Falls retired in 1960 after serving 39 years as principal. In the photograph above, Dr. Falls speaks with teachers during a faculty meeting. Pictured below are teachers Joseph Simmons and John Strong, Jr., serving as Boy Scout masters for a troop at Geeter High School. (Courtesy of Collection of Rev. Dr. Clennon Saulsberry, Sr.)

Pictured left is Dr. Montee Falls, wife of Dr. Joseph W. Falls. A Tennessee A & I State University graduate, Dr. Falls served as a teacher at Geeter for more than 30 years. During the late 1930s, their daughter, Mildred Falls Davis, began teaching at Geeter. Dr. Falls and her husband both served as ministers of the Unity Center of Memphis. (Courtesy of Collection of Rev. Dr. Clennon Saulsberry, Sr.)

Torris Jacob "T.J." Toney was the principal of Geeter High School from 1960 to 1972. He earned a bachelor's degree from LeMoyne College and a master's from the Tuskegee Institute in 1960. Before being appointed principal of Geeter, Toney was a teacher at Woodstock School, principal of Weaver Elementary, and assistant principal at Geeter High. A community servant, he proudly served his community through his church, Mt. Olive CME Church, and Alpha Phi Alpha Fraternity, Inc. He retired from Memphis City Schools in 1972. (Courtesy of Collection of Rev. Dr. Clennon Saulsberry, Sr.)

Geraldine Sims taught at Geeter High School in the 1930s. She retired in 1961 as a teacher at Douglass High School and taught in Mississippi, Louisiana, and Memphis for 50 years. She graduated from Alcorn State College in Alcorn, MS, and her husband, Professor Benjamin W. Sims, was a principal in West Memphis, AR. (Courtesy of a private collection)

# BOOKER T. WASHINGTON HIGH SCHOOL

Booker T. Washington (B.T.W.) High School is a descendant of the Clay Street School that was established in the late 1860s to serve the African American children of the city of Memphis. The school, pictured below, was located on Clay Street and was named after Henry Clay, who served as the United States Secretary of State and Senator from Kentucky. The street would be renamed St. Paul Street several years later. The first Clay Street School building was a two-room wooden structure with two teachers. Leaders of the city of Memphis allocated funds for a new Clay Street School to be built to replace one in a state of disrepair. This building would be the first all-brick school building in the city for its African American students. It contained eight classrooms, was furnished with new furniture, and was equipped with the common amenities of the time. In the late 1870s, the school on Clay Street was renamed Kortrecht Grammar School after Memphis Public Schools Board President Charles Kortrecht. The photograph below shows Kortrecht School on Clay Street when the grammar and high school occupied the same building. (Courtesy of a private collection)

In 1876, Mr. Benjamin K. Sampson was appointed principal. He was the first African American principal of a public school in Memphis. In 1908, the following teachers made up the school's faculty: G.P Hamilton, Principal, E.L. Honesty, Grammar School Principal, S.A. Haynes, Aleda E. Jones, M.L. Jones, Mary E. Hall, Maggie B. Cox, Barnetta Glodsby, N.E. Whiteman, Maud E. Mosby, Annie L. Taylor, Beatrice Robinson, Hannah Wilson, Emma L. Crittenden, and Sadie L. Saunders. After serving thousands of students for several years, the building began showing significant deterioration. In 1911, city leaders moved Kortrecht High School into the old Peabody School building that was vacated when Peabody moved into its new building at 2086 Young Ave., which is still in use today. In 1926, the school relocated from its site near a railyard to a new building at 715 South Lauderdale and was renamed Booker T. Washington High School. Pictured above is the B.T.W. Junior Band. The photograph below shows students in a formation spelling "B.T.W." on the school's football field. (Courtesy of a private collection)

Green Polonius Hamilton was the principal of Booker T. Washington High School from 1892 until he died in 1932. Professor Hamilton was born in Memphis in 1867. He attended the LeMoyne Normal Institute in Memphis, Rust College in Holly Springs, Mississippi, and then Columbia University in New York. Hamilton returned to Memphis and began teaching in public schools in 1884. He started the first African American high school band in the city. Professor Hamilton also authored two books, *The Bright Side of Memphis* (1908) and *Beacon Lights of the Race* (1911). Hamilton K-8 and High Schools in Memphis are named in his honor. (Courtesy of the Tennessee State University Special Collection)

Blair Theodore Hunt, Jr. was the second principal of Booker T. Washington High School and was the principal for 24 years from 1932 until 1956. Professor Hunt attended the LeMoyne Normal Institute, Morehouse College, Tennessee A & I State University, and Harvard University. After college, he returned to Memphis in 1913, where he took a teaching position at Porter Jr. High School with the Memphis City School District. He served overseas in the US Army during WWI and returned a few years later. Before being named principal of Booker T. Washington High, Professor Hunt served as principal of the LaRose School. Blair T. Hunt was also a member of Alpha Phi Alpha Fraternity, Inc. (Courtesy of a private collection)

Pictured left is Herschel C. Latham. A graduate of Talladega College in Talladega, AL, and the Bradley Institute in Peoria, IL, Professor Latham served as the woodwork teacher at Booker T. Washington High School for seventeen years from 1927 to 1944. In 1944, he left public education to enter the undertaker business. He was a member of Alpha Phi Alpha Fraternity, Inc. (Courtesy of a private collection)

Lucie Eddie Campbell-Williams, pictured left, was an educator, composer, and activist. She began her teaching career at Carnes Avenue School in 1900. She taught at Carnes School until 1911. In 1911, she was appointed to teach at Kortrecht High School. She would remain at the school until her retirement in 1954. Mrs. Campbell-Williams was a 1927 graduate of Rust College and Tennessee A & I State College, earning a master's degree in 1951. She was best known as a great gospel composer who worked with musical talents such as Marian Anderson, Thomas A. Dorsey, and Mahalia Jackson. Lucie E. Campbell Elementary School in Memphis is named in her honor. (Courtesy of a private collection)

Dr. Wendell P. Whalum, pictured left as a high school student, was a 1948 Booker T. Washington High School graduate. Dr. Whalum earned a Bachelor of Arts degree from Morehouse College in 1952, a Master of Arts degree from Columbia University in 1953, and a Doctor of Philosophy degree from the University of Iowa in 1965. In 1953, he was named the director of the Morehouse College Glee Club, a position he held for over 30 years. At Morehouse College, he served as conductor and organist for several Atlanta Churches and was a highly sought-after arranger, composer, and lecturer. He was a member of Phi Beta Kappa and Alpha Phi Alpha Fraternity, Inc. (Courtesy of a private collection)

William Theodore McDaniel was a teacher and band director at Booker T. Washington High. He began his teaching career in Tupelo, MS in 1927. His teaching career in Memphis began in 1941. During his time in Memphis, he served as the band director for both Manassas High and Booker T. Washington High School until 1948, when he decided to focus solely on the development of the Booker T. Washington High Band. "Mr. Mac" was a 1927 graduate of Rust College, where he was classmates with fellow B.T.W. High School Teacher Lucie E. Campbell-Williams. He remained at Booker T. Washington until 1958. He was a member of Alpha Phi Alpha, Fraternity, Inc. (Courtesy of a private collection)

Jesse Dozzell Springer, pictured left, was named principal of Booker T. Washington High School in 1959. His appointment as principal followed the retirement of principal Blair T. Hunt. Before arriving at B.T.W., Professor Springer taught at the school for 14 years. Additionally, he served as the principal of Melrose High School for five years and Douglass High School for eight years, from 1951 to 1959. He served as the Memphis City Schools Co-Coordinator of Negro Education for two years before arriving at Douglass High. Principal Springer was a 1926 graduate of Howard University, earning a Bachelor of Science and a Master of Arts from Columbia University. (Courtesy of a private collection)

Mose Walker, Jr., pictured left, was a graduate and principal of Booker T. Washington High School. He graduated from B.T.W. in 1951. Mr. Walker earned a Bachelor of Science Degree from LeMoyne College in 1955 and a Master of Arts from Fisk University in 1962. Mr. Walker began his career in 1957 as a biology teacher at Douglass High School. He was appointed assistant principal of his alma mater, Booker T. Washington High, in 1963. In 1968, he was appointed principal of Lincoln Jr. High School. From 1970 until his passing in 1986, he served as the principal of Booker T. Washington High School. He was a member of Omega Psi Phi Fraternity, Inc. (Courtesy of a private collection)

Nathaniel Dowd "Nat D." Williams. served as a history teacher at Booker T. Washington for 43 years. Born in Memphis, Professor Williams earned a Bachelor of Science degree in 1928 and a Master of Science in 1956 from Tennessee A & I State College. Williams may be most remembered for his writing for the Memphis World and Tri-State Defender Newspapers, serving as the host for the famed Amateur Night on Beale Street, co-founding the city's Cotton Makers Jubilee, and serving as the first African American disc jockey in Memphis when he signed on for the new WDIA Radio Station in 1948. As a teacher, Williams inspired the likes of Benjamin Hooks and Dr. Willie W. Herenton. As host of Beale Street's Amateur Night and WDIA Disc Jockey, he helped to make Rufus Thomas, B.B. King, and Bobby "Blue" Bland stars. (Courtesy of a private collection)

# MELROSE HIGH SCHOOL
# (ROSENWALD)

The first Melrose School was established in 1890 in Melrose Station, just outside Memphis limits. The original school was a simple two-story building. Shortly after opening, the school was renamed after Dr. Melrose, a wealthy philanthropist who gave money and support to many school and community activities. Below is a photograph of the two-story Melrose School Building at 843 Dallas Street. The picture above is the Melrose School building that was built in 1914. (Courtesy of the Memphis Public Library & Information Center)

**MELROSE**
*The 1st Negro Junior High School in Memphis, Tenn.*
1. The Old Building        2. The New Building
R. H. Neville, Principal, (Inset)

Over time, the old two-story frame structure became dangerous and needed help to support the growing student population. In 1936, the Memphis City School Board decided to replace the old structure with a new, modern building. The Memphis Press-Scimitar stated that the school would be "fireproof." Once completed in 1938, the smaller Park Avenue School at 846 Maywood was closed and merged with Melrose. The school would serve grades first through eight until 1946. Principal Richard H. Neville served as the school's principal until 1949 when Floyd M. Campbell was appointed principal of Melrose. Professor Campbell would remain the principal for 20 years. In 1969, Melvin N. Conley was appointed Melrose High School principal, and he remained there until 1979, when LaVaughn Bridges was named principal. Above is a postcard featuring the new and old Melrose buildings and Principal R.H. Neville. (Courtesy of The University of Memphis Special Collection) Below is a biology class led by Ruthie Campbell Strong in the 1950's. (Courtesy of a private collection)

Pictured left is Principal Richard H. Neville. Professor Neville was a graduate of the LeMoyne Normal Institute. He was an educator in Memphis and rural Shelby County, serving as a teacher at Carnes School before his appointment to principal of Greenwood School, Melrose High School, and Klondike Elementary. Principal Neville served as the principal of Melrose School during the transition from the original two-story, wood frame building to the new two-story brick building on Dallas Street in Orange Mound. Professor Neville also served as principal of Neshoba Jr. High School in Germantown, Tennessee, as an educator. (Courtesy of the Tennessee State University Special Collection)

FLOYD M. CAMPBELL

Principal Floyd M. Campbell served as the principal of Melrose High School for twenty years, from 1949 to 1969. He graduated from Morehouse College in Atlanta and earned a master's degree from Atlanta University. He served as a teacher at Manassas High School in Memphis before being appointed the principal of Kortrecht Intermediate School and Porter Jr. High School. During his time as principal, the Melrose Football Team won five consecutive state championships from 1953 to 1957. He was a member of Kappa Alpha Psi Fraternity, Inc. (Courtesy of a private collection)

Pictured left is Ruthie Campbell Strong in the mid-1950s. In her 30 plus years at Melrose, Mrs. Strong served as a teacher, guidance counselor, and assistant principal. Strong was a 1951 graduate of Manassas High School. After high school, she earned a Bachelor of Science degree in Biology from Lane College in 1955, a Master of Education degree in Educational Guidance from Tennessee State University in 1960, and an Education Specialist degree from the University of Tennessee at Knoxville. Mrs. Strong was a member of Delta Sigma Theta Sorority, Inc. and the wife of longtime Woodstock School Principal John E. Strong, Jr. (Courtesy of a private collection)

Pictured left is Dr. Willie E. Lindsey, who served as a math teacher at Melrose for several years. Dr. Lindsey was a 1948 graduate of Booker T. Washington High School. Following high school, he earned a Bachelor of Science degree from Arkansas M & N College in 1952, a Master of Science from Tennessee State University in 1959, an Ed.D. from the University of Tennessee at Knoxville, and a Ph.D. from the University of Delaware. Dr. Lindsey also served as a guidance counselor at Overton High School and as Assistant Principal at Hamilton High School and Northside High School. He was a member of Alpha Phi Alpha Fraternity, Inc. (Courtesy of a private collection)

Dr. Joseph Wilson Westbrook III was a teacher and coach at Melrose High School from 1944 to 1959. A graduate of Manassas High School, he attended LeMoyne College and graduated in 1943. He earned a Master of Science Degree in Educational Supervision in 1961 from Tennessee State University and a Ph.D. from the University of Tennessee. In 1944, he was hired as a teacher at Melrose High School, where he taught physics and chemistry and coached football, basketball, and track. The football teams he led were some of the most successful in the Memphis School history. In 1959, he was appointed an assistant principal at Booker T. Washington High School, where he also coached. He was appointed the first African American supervisor of secondary instruction in Memphis City Schools history in 1963 and became area superintendent in 1971. He retired in 1981. He was a member of Alpha Phi Alpha Fraternity, Inc. (Courtesy of a private collection)

# HAMILTON HIGH SCHOOL

The first Hamilton School, established around 1866 near Heistan Place and South Bellevue Boulevard in the Greenwood Station area of Memphis, was named the Greenwood School. It officially became part of the Memphis City School District in 1899. In 1909, a new school building for Greenwood opened at 993 Melrose Street. Pictured above is the building that opened in 1941 at 1478 Wilson St. Photo above courtesy of The University of Memphis Special Collection. The photograph below shows students and a teacher in a classroom at Hamilton High in the 1940's. (Courtesy of The University of Memphis Special Collection)

Hamilton originally opened in 1941 as a Junior High School. When it opened, this new building replaced Memphis's last large, two-story wood frame school building. In 1943, the Memphis City School Board approved the school to be renamed Hamilton High School after the late Booker T. Washington High School Principal, G.P. Hamilton. The school's first senior class graduated in 1945. Pictured above is of the 1947 Homecoming Queen with football team members. (Courtesy of a private collection)

Principal James Lowell Buckner began his career in education as a teacher at Kortrecht High School in 1914. According to the Commercial Appeal, he served as a teacher at Manassas School and the principal of Magnolia, Hyde Park, Kortrecht Grammar, and Carnes Schools before being appointed to Greenwood School in 1942. He retired in 1953 after 40 years of Memphis City School District service. (Courtesy of the Tennessee State University Special Collection)

Dr. Harry T. Cash, left, was appointed principal of Hamilton High School in 1953 when James Lowell Buckner retired. Dr. Cash would hold that title until his retirement in 1969. Before his time at Hamilton High, Cash was a teacher at Grant Elementary and the principal of Porter Jr. High School. A graduate of LeMoyne High School, he earned a Bachelor of Science degree from Lane College in 1937 and a Master of Science degree from Tennessee A & I State College in 1947. Dr. Cash received his doctoral degree from Lane College. In addition to his 40 years of service to public schools in Memphis, Dr. Cash co-founded Tri-State Boxing, which promoted amateur boxing for the National Golden Gloves Tournament. (Courtesy of the Tennessee State University Special Collection)

Dr. Lulah McEwen Hedgeman was a student and teacher at Hamilton High School. As a high school sophomore, she was chosen by the Ford Foundation for early college admission based on her exceptional test scores. She graduated from Fisk University in 1959 with a Bachelor of Arts in Music and earned a Master of Music degree from Memphis State University in 1970. After graduating from Fisk, she accepted a teaching position at Melrose. She relocated to Chicago for a short period before returning to Memphis to teach vocal music at Hamilton High School in the 1960s. She accepted the vocal music teaching position at Treadwell High School in 1970 before becoming the vocal music director at Overton High School in 1976, where she spent the remainder of her teaching career. A member of Delta Sigma Theta Sorority, Inc., she received the Honorary Doctor of Fine Arts degree from Rhodes College in 1994. (Courtesy of a private collection)

# MITCHELL ROAD HIGH SCHOOL

Mitchell Road High School opened on Mitchell Road in 1957. The new 18-room, two-story school building opened to relieve overcrowding at Ford Road and Weaver Schools and the growth of Walker Homes Community. Mr. Alonzo Weaver, former principal at Weaver School, was appointed the first principal of Mitchell High. Mr. Weaver served as the principal of Mitchell until his retirement in 1979. Mr. Weaver earned a Bachelor of Science Degree from LeMoyne College in 1942 and earned a Master of Science Degree in Administration and Supervision from Tennessee State University in 1962. Before he arrived at Mitchell High, he served as a teacher and principal at Weaver Elementary School. Mr. Weaver was a member of Alpha Phi Alpha Fraternity, Inc. Mitchell's first senior class graduated in 1961. In 1963, the Memphis City School District built a 12-room addition and library on the school's campus. Alfred Motlow, Sr. became the second principal to serve at Mitchell High School when Mr. Weaver retired in 1979. Mr. Motlow is a 1954 Booker T. Washington High School graduate, and the brother of Memphis educator Floyd Harrison, Jr. Mr. Motlow first attended Fisk University for two years, where he was a member of the famed Fisk Jubilee Singers. Motlow went on to graduate from Tennessee State University in 1958, where he earned a Bachelor of Science Degree in Elementary Education, and he also earned a Master of Education Degree in Guidance and Counseling from Memphis State University. He began his career in education as a teacher at Douglass High School. In 1972, he was appointed an assistant principal of Hamilton High School. In 1979, he was appointed principal of Mitchell High School following the retirement of the school's first principal, Alonzo Weaver, Sr. Mr. Motlow is a member of Omega Psi Phi Fraternity, Inc. Since the school's opening in 1957, building additions to the school were made in the following years: 1958; 1962; 1964; 1976, 1977, and 1998. In 2002, a new 45-room, air conditioned building was completed. Mitchell High School remains an active school. (Courtesy of a private collection)

# CAPLEVILLE HIGH SCHOOL

In the early days of the Capleville Community, there were two Capleville Schools. Capleville-78, situated on present-day Highway 78, served white students, and Capleville-Shelby, once located at 4344 East Shelby Drive near present-day Shelby Drive and Malone Rd., was for African American students. The first Capleville School for African Americans was built sometime before 1912. In 1923, a new Rosenwald School Building was constructed. At this time, the school was outside of the city limits. In the 1950s, the school consisted of two buildings: one frame and the other brick veneer. Elizabeth N. Townsend was principal of Capleville School during the 1940s. She was promoted to supervisor in 1951, and Ezra L. Ford was named the new principal. In 1964, John Strong, Jr. was named the principal. He held that title until 1966 when he was appointed the principal of the Woodstock School. Replacing Principal Strong was Joseph Simmons. He remained at Capleville School until 1970, when the Capleville-78 School closed, and Capleville-Shelby became an integrated school. The school suffered significant fire damage in 2009, and the remaining portion of the structure was demolished. The picture above is of Capleville High School in the 1970's. The photo below is the school years after closing its doors. (Courtesy of a private collection)

Ezra Laval Ford was appointed the principal of Capleville High School in 1951. He attended Tennessee A & I State College for three years before enlisting in the United States Army during WWII in 1942. When his service ended in 1945, Ford resumed his studies at LeMoyne College and graduated in 1947 with a Bachelor of Science. He also earned a Master of Science in Administration and Supervision from Tennessee State University in 1961. He was hired as a teacher at Barret's Chapel High School in 1948. His wife, Rosa Ford, a Manassas High and LeMoyne College graduate, also taught for the Memphis City School District. (Courtesy of a private collection)

Mrs. Elizabeth Townsend was the principal of the Capleville School before Ezra Ford. She was a 1939 graduate of LeMoyne College, where she earned a Bachelor of Science degree, and she earned a Master of Science degree in Educational Supervision from Tennessee A & I State College in 1952. In 1951, she was appointed the Shelby County Jeanes Supervisor for Negro School. As the county supervisor, she was responsible for improving teaching and learning in the county's African American schools. (Courtesy of the Tennessee State University Special Collection)

# CARVER HIGH SCHOOL

George Washington Carver High School opened in 1957 junior high as a school for African American students in the community bordered by Riverside, Lauderdale, and South Parkway. When the school opened, it served grades seven through nine, and another grade was added each year until students entered grade twelve in 1960. The first senior class graduated in 1961. The first principal of G.W. Carver was Richard B. Thompson. When the school opened in September of 1961, the school was unfinished. Pictured above and below is the building that opened in 1957. (Courtesy of a private collection)

For the first two months of the school's opening, parents in the community supported the students with lunches because the cafeteria was completed in November. When completed, G.W. Carver had a 1,000-seat gym, 30 classrooms, a library, science labs, and rooms for shops and the arts. By 1960, over 2,200 students were enrolled at the school.

Former Memphis City Schools Superintendent Johnnie B. Watson was a guidance counselor at Carver High in the early 1960's. He graduated from Booker T. Washington High School and earned a Bachelor of Arts from LeMoyne College in 1960. He also earned a master's degree from Indiana University in 1966. In 1968, he was appointed to a central office position within the Memphis City School district. Between 1968 and his retirement in 1992, Mr. Watson served as a counselor, assistant superintendent, and deputy superintendent. Upon retiring in 1992, he accepted the position of chair of the department of education and distinguished associate professor at Rhodes College. Watson returned to Memphis City Schools in 2001 after being named superintendent. He served the district in this role until 2003. He was appointed president of his alma mater, LeMoyne Owen College, in 2008 and served in the college until 2015. He is an active member of Alpha Phi Alpha Fraternity, Inc.

Frances Dancy Hooks was head of the guidance department at the new George Washington Carver High School. Mrs. Hooks was a 1944 graduate of Booker T. Washington High School. After high school, she attended Howard and Wilberforce Universities before enrolling and majoring in education at Fisk University, where she earned a Bachelor of Science degree in 1949. 1968, she earned a Master of Science degree in Guidance and Counseling from Tennessee State University. Her first teaching assignment was at Barret's Chapel High School as a Physical Education Teacher and coach in 1949. She also taught at Mt. Pisgah before accepting a position at Carver High. She left public education to work alongside her husband, civil rights attorney and executive director of the NAACP, Benjamin Hooks. She was a member of Delta Sigma Theta Sorority, Inc.

After serving the South Memphis for 59 years, Carver High School closed in 2016. It currently serves as the G.W. Carver College and Career Academy. (Courtesy of a private collection)

Pictured is Richard B. Thompson, the first principal of George Washington Carver High School. He was named principal of G.W. Carver in 1957 and served until his retirement in 1975. Principal Thompson began his tenure in Memphis in 1945 when he was elected to a teacher position at Porter Jr. High School. In 1952, he was appointed principal of Grant School in North Memphis, where he served until 1957. (Courtesy of a private collection)

Herman R. Rankins was the Carver High School Band director from 1958 to 1979. Known to many as "The Mastero," Mr. Rankins graduated from Manassas High School and earned a bachelor's degree from Arkansas AM&N. He led the marching, concert, and jazz bands while allowing his students to perform in the Cotton Makers Jubilee and Cotton Carnival Parades. He was a member of Alpha Phi Alpha Fraternity, Inc. (Courtesy of a private collection)

James Howard Black, pictured left, was a history teacher during the early days of George Washington Carver High School. After graduating from Manassas High School, he earned a bachelor's degree from LeMoyne College in 1952 and a Master of Education degree from Memphis State University in 1970. Black began his career in education as a teacher at Riverview Elementary. He left Carver High when he was appointed assistant principal of South Side High School. In 1976, he was appointed principal of Messick Jr. High School. Principal Black accepted the same role at Florida Elementary in 1977. (Courtesy of a private collection)

# PORTER JR. HIGH SCHOOL

The first Porter School opened around 1885 at 646 Georgia Ave. In 1893, the Commercial Appeal named Charles A. Thompson as the school's principal. In 1910, Phillip Alexander Dickerson served as the principal of Porter. Several years later, James M. Jones, serving as principal, died in 1919, and Samuel S. Brown was appointed acting principal. In September of 1919, Lawyer E. Brown was pointed principal. He remained the principal of Porter School until his retirement in 1946. Construction of a new Porter School building was approved by the Memphis Public School Board in 1922. The new building was a two-story structure with 14 classrooms, a large auditorium, a manual training department, a cafeteria, playrooms, a teacher's workroom, and a nurse's clinic. Pictured above is Porter School in the mid-1930s. (Courtesy of a private collection) Below are the students and staff of Porter School in the 1940's. Professor Lawyer E. Brown is standing on the far left with the Foote Homes Housing Project in the background. (Courtesy of the Memphis Public Library & Information Center)

Mr. Floyd Campbell was appointed the principal of Porter when Lawyer E. Brown retired in 1946. When Mr. Campbell was named principal of Melrose High in 1949, Mr. Harry T. Cash was named principal of the Porter. Richard B. Thompson was named Porter's principal in 1953 after Mr. Cash was named principal of Hamilton High. In 1954, a new school building for Porter was constructed and opened. The new structure was a three-story, 25-classroom building with music rooms, labs, and shops. That year, Porter School became the first junior high school for African American students in Memphis. Melvin Conley was named principal in 1957 when Principal Thompson was appointed to the new Carver High, and he remained at Porter until 1959. Pictured above is a classroom with students and a teacher at Porter School in 1943. (Courtesy of the Tennessee State University Special Collection)

Pictured left is Porter School Principal, Lawyer E. Brown. Professor Brown was appointed principal in 1919 and served as principal until his retirement in 1946. A LeMoyne Institute and Fisk University graduate, Brown taught in Memphis for 52 years before retiring. Before his time at Porter School, he served as the principal of the Greenwood School and LaRose Street School. Following his death in 1947, a park in his honor sits near the old Porter Jr. High School building. (Courtesy of the Tennessee State University Special Collection)

Abner Bernard "A.B." Owen, Jr. was the principal of Porter Jr. High School from 1959 until his sudden passing in 1968. Professor Owen attended the LeMoyne Normal Institute before earning Bachelor of Art and Master of Art degrees from Fisk University in Nashville, Tennessee. Before his time at Porter, he taught at Alonzo Locke Elementary and was the principal of Kortrecht Elementary and Kansas Elementary. Principal Owen was a member of Alpha Phi Alpha Fraternity, Inc. (Courtesy of the Tennessee State University Special Collection)

Pictured right is Othella Sawyer Shannon who served as the principal of the elementary portion of Porter Jr. High from 1956 to 1961. Mrs. Shannon was a 1934 graduate of LeMoynce College and did graduate work at the Chicago Normal Institute and Ohio State University. She previously taught mathematics and science at Hamilton High School and Porter before being appointed co-principal. In 1961, she was named the first principal of the new Georgia Avenue Elementary School. She remained the school's principal until her retirement in 1976. Principal Sawyer was a member of Delta Sigma Theta Sorority, Inc. (Courtesy of a private collection)

# KORTRECHT GRAMMAR SCHOOL

Kortrecht Grammar School began as the Clay Street School and opened in the late 1860s. In 1873, Clay Street School, renamed Kortrecht School years later for Memphis Public School Board President Charles Kortrecht, became the first brick school building constructed for African Americans in the city of Memphis. The building was a two-story building with eight rooms. The name "Clay Street Public School" was on the east side of the building. Years later, Clay Street was renamed St. Paul Avenue. The 1939 map image below shows the Kortrecht Grammar School circled. The school was bordered by Calhoun (now named G.E. Patterson) to the North, Webster Avenue to the South, Fourth Street to the East, and Hernando Street to the West. The property that the school stood on is across the street from the present-day Temple of Deliverance Church of God in Christ Cathedral. (Courtesy of the Memphis Public Library & Information Center)

In 1908, E.L. Honesty was the school's principal, and the school had a total of 16 teachers and an enrolment of 850 students. Professor Daniel W. Gary was appointed principal after Professor Honesty left Kortrecht. Gary earned a Bachelor of Science in English from Alcorn A & M College. He also taught civics and history at Alcorn before accepting a position to teach in Memphis. In 1926, the following teachers and staff made up the faculty of Kortrecht Grammar: Hannah Atwood, Adrean Blackburn, Mary Bradford, Annette Brown, Estelle Campbell, Edna May Clark, Emma L. Coleman, Sarah Davis, Willette Downs, Jessie C. Gwyn, Victoria G. Mays, Darthula Hodges, Mattye Porter, Annette Russell, Bennie G. Sampson, Jeanetta Shivers, Nettie Smith, Velma Gavin Thomas, Sarah Martin White, Nannie E. Whiteman, Assistant Principal, Sadie L. Williams, Amanda Woodfin, and W.O. Worrell. The following teachers made up the faculty of Kortrecht Grammar in 1936: Leslie H. Taylor, Bennie Booth, Mary Bradford, Annette Brown, Estelle Campbell, Sarah Davis, Jessie C. Gwynn, Lillian Maxey, Victoria G. Mays, Lillian Peck, Mattye Porter, Imogene Powers, Sarah Martin, and Sadie L. Williams. Shortly after Booker T. Washington High School was opened, Kortrecht Grammar moved into the old high school building on Webster Street, abandoning the building on St. Paul Street. In 1943, the old Krotrecht Grammar School, which was no longer in use, was repurposed as a workshop for the blind. The Memphis City School District sold the property, and the building was torn down years later. (Courtesy of a private collection)

Edward Lincoln Honesty, pictured left, served as the principal of Kortrecht Grammar School during the early 1900's and 1910's. He graduated from Mechanicsburg High School and Oberlin College in Ohio and served as teacher and principal for over 50 years. In 1892, he was appointed the assistant of Kortrecht High School principal, G.P. Hamilton. He retired as the principal of Grant School in Memphis. (Courtesy of a private collection)

# KORTRECHT INTERMEDIATE SCHOOL

The Kortrecht Intermediate School was housed in the old Peabody School on Webster Avenue and Second Street. The building was named after financier and philanthropist George Peabody, who donated funds to the Memphis Public School District for the school. It was constructed in 1873 and was bordered by Grand Central Station on the West, Union Station on the East, Georgia Avenue to the South, and Calhoun Avenue to the North, as seen in the 1939 map image below. The photograph above is of the school building when Peabody School occupied it. (Courtesy of a private collection)

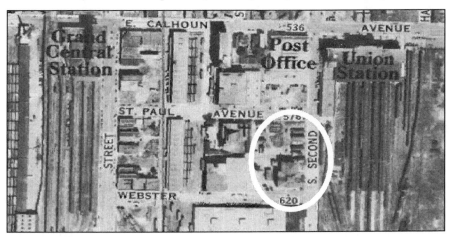

In 1936, the following teachers made up the faculty at Kortrecht Intermediate the same year: J.L. Buckner, Principal; Emma L. Coleman, Herman B. King, Blanche E. Neal, Walter L. Pamphlett, Pearl V. Range, Elizabeth H. Wallace, and Amanda Woodfin. Pictured above is Kortrecht Intermediate on Webster Avenue. Mr. Floyd M. Campbell was appointed principal of Kortrecht after Mr. Buckner was named principal of Greenwood School (Hamilton). In 1952, Elizabeth H. Wallace was the school's principal. The following teachers made up the faculty in 1952: Mrs. Mollie J. Carter, Miss Frankie L. Cash, Mrs. Dan E. Gurley, Mrs. Christabel P. Johnson, Mrs. Esther A. Jones, Mr. Thomas L. McClellan, Mrs. Helen B. Miller, Miss Vashti L. Montague, Miss Blanche Neal, and Mr. John L. Outlaw. After the death of Principal Wallace in 1954, the following principals led Kortrecht: Mildred T. Carver (1954-1956), Helen Hooks (1956-1957), Abner B. Owen (1957-1958), William "Tiny" Cox (1958-1959), Theodore R. Johnson (1959-1960), and Bennie M. Batts (1960-1961). Kortrecht closed in 1961, and the school district sold the property to the Yellow Cab Co. in 1965. The school building was demolished in 1966. (Courtesy of a private collection)

Elizabeth H. Wallace, pictured left, was the principal of Kortrecht Intermediate School from 1945 until she died in 1954. Miss Wallace served as a teacher at Kortrecht for several years before being appointed the school's principal. She was an accomplished musician and attended the Minnesota School of Music in the late 1920s. (Courtesy of the Tennessee State University Special Collection)

Bennie Marshall Batts, pictured right, served as the last principal of Kortrecht Intermediate School. Appointed in 1960, Mr. Batts served as the school's teaching principal. He came to Kortrecht from Lester Elementary, where he served as a teacher for 7 years. Principal Batts earned a Bachelor of Arts degree from Tennessee A & I State College in 1947 and a Master of Arts from Memphis State University in 1963. In 1961, he was named principal of Lincoln Elementary, where he remained until 1969 when he was appointed principal of Caldwell Elementary. Mr. Batts was a member of Kappa Alpha Psi Fraternity, Inc. (Courtesy of the Tennessee State University Special Collection)

# MAGNOLIA ELEMENTARY SCHOOL
## (ROSENWALD)

Magnolia Elementary School was a very early school in Southwest Shelby County. The first known public school established in the Magnolia and Castalia Heights area was built by the Memphis Public School District around 1917. Pictured above and below are photographs of the Magnolia Elementary School (with coal-burning stoves) in 1948 before renovations were completed. (Courtesy of the Memphis Public Library & Information Center)

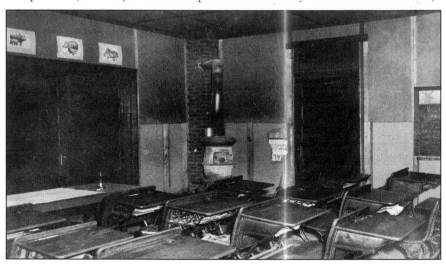

Magnolia School was among Memphis's first schools to serve the Castalia Heights Community. The school was first mentioned in a 1924 article in the Commercial Appeal Newspaper. James Lovell Buckner served as the principal of Magnolia Elementary School at this time. He went on to become the principal of Hamilton High School. Mary E. Murphy followed Professor Buckner as the principal around 1926. She remained the principal of Magnolia until 1947 when she was transferred to Alonzo Locke School. Pictured above is a renovated classroom at Magnolia Elementary School in the late 1940's or early 1950's. (Courtesy of the Memphis Public Library & Information Center) Pictured below is the exterior of the twenty-two-teacher school located at 2061 Livewell Circle. (Courtesy of the Tennessee State University Special Collection)

Pictured left is Harry Mae Simons. For 33 years, from 1947 to 1980, she served as the principal of Magnolia Elementary School. She graduated from LeMoyne College and Tennessee A & I State College. Before their time at Magnolia, she served as a teacher at LaRose Elementary. Dr. Willie W. Herenton, the former superintendent of Memphis City Schools and Mayor of Memphis, was one of her students. During her tenure as Magnolia's principal, she served as the president of the WTEC from 1952 to 1954. A member of the Sigma Gamma Rho Sorority and an active community leader, she retired in 1980 after thirty-six years as an educator in Memphis. (Courtesy of the Tennessee State University Special Collection)

Principal Simons went to great lengths to ensure Magnolia School teachers had all they needed to help students reach their goals. The picture below was featured in the March 1951 issue of The Broadcaster, the official journal of the Tennessee Negro Education Association. The teachers' lounge was decorated with upholstered furniture, lamps, tables, and a work desk. Additionally, charts with teaching strategies shared during teacher in-service hung in the lounge for teachers to review. In that issue of The Broadcaster, Magnolia was called "a laboratory, a delightful place, where adjustment, growth, and happiness go hand in hand." Magnolia Elementary closed and merged with the new Alcy Elementary in 2021. (Courtesy of the Tennessee State University Special Collection)

# LAROSE SCHOOL

Larose School is one of the oldest schools in Memphis that is still in operation. The first Larose School can be traced back to around 1911. A 1919 government report on the public schools in Memphis reported that the original LaRose School building accommodated only eight classes, but 27 were present. Portable buildings housed the extra classes, but the rooms were extremely overcrowded. The report noted that nearly 90 children occupied a room meant for 50 in some rooms. In 1922, a new LaRose School building for the children in the community around S. Wellington Street was erected. One of the first principals of the school was Professor James D. Cotton. Professor Cotton taught in Memphis and West Tennessee for nearly 40 years. When he died in 1926, the community came together to make the arrangements for Principal Cotton. By the early 1950s, Larose School was one of the largest grammar schools in Shelby County, with over 1,400 students. The image above is of Larose School around 1922. (Courtesy of the Memphis Public Library & Information Center)

Pictured above is the faculty of Larose Elementary in 1952. The teachers at Larose School that year were: Front Row: Mr. Adams Barley, Mrs. Bessie Rice, Mrs. Cora Leatherwood, Mrs. Pearl Clark, Mrs. Zenobia Merriweather, Principal John L. Brinkley, Mrs. Mattie Goldsby, Miss Eloise Bacon, Miss Mary Range, Mrs. Evelyn Taylor, Mr. Garmer Currie, Sr. Second row: Miss Gertrude Walker, Mrs. Esther Brown, Mrs. Thelma Motley, Mrs. Josie Flowers, Miss Eva Broome, Mrs. Erie Rose, Mrs. Jessie Presley, Miss Ophelia Watson, Miss Willean Freeman. Third Row: Miss Marilyn Watkins, Mrs. Daisy Cartwright, Mrs. Elizabeth Cox, Miss Geraldine Davis, Mrs. Minnie Lincoln, Mrs. Cleora Neale, Mrs. Willie M. Broome, Miss Ruth Holmes, Mrs. Mattie Tyus. Back Row: Mrs. Leath Jones, Mrs. Josie Cobb, Mrs. Eugenia Danner, Miss Mary McGuire, Miss Geraldine Gray, Mrs. Dorothy Bryant. Mrs. Nellie Roulhac, Miss Allison Vance, and Miss Jacqueline Flowers were not pictured. (Courtesy of the Tennessee State University Special Collection)

Dr. Willie W. Herenton attended Larose Elementary and Booker T. Washington High School. After graduating from LeMoyne College, he was a fifth-grade teacher at Shannon Elementary. At the age of 28, Dr. Herenton was appointed the principal of Larose Elementary, making him the youngest principal to be hired in Memphis City Schools at the time. In 1966, Herenton earned a Master of Arts degree from Memphis State University. A few years later, earned a Doctor of Philosophy degree from Southern Illinois University in 1971 and was named superintendent of Memphis City Schools in 1979. In 1991, he made history by becoming Memphis's first elected African American mayor.

One of the principals at Larose School was Edwin Chappelle "E.C." Jones. Professor Chappelle was a native Memphian who attended Wilberforce University before beginning his teaching career in North Carolina. He returned to Memphis in the 1920s and was hired as a science teacher at Booker T. Washington High School. Jones became the principal of Larose School in the early 1932 when Blair T. Hunt was appointed the principal at Booker T. Washington following the death of G.P. Hamilton. He stayed at Larose until he was appointed the principal of Carnes School in 1945. He was a member of Alpha Phi Alpha Fraternity, Inc. (Courtesy of a private collection)

John Lewis Brinkley, Jr. served as the principal of Larose School for 25 years, from 1945 to 1970. Professor Brinkley was a graduate of Wilberforce University in Ohio. After completing his undergraduate studies, he returned to Memphis, first teaching at LeMoyne College. After a few years at LeMoyne, he taught at Kortrecht Grammar School, Booker T. Washington High School, and Manassas High School. He was named principal in 1945 when Principal E C. Jones was appointed the principal at Carnes Avenue School. Principal Brinkley, a member of Alpha Phi Alpha Fraternity, Inc., retired in 1970 with forty years of service to Memphis City Schools. (Courtesy of a private collection)

# WHITE'S CHAPEL SCHOOL
# (ROSENWALD)

White's Chapel School was located at 3966 Sewanee Road, just South of Fields Road in the Boxtown Community. White's Chapel School was first mentioned in the Commercial Appeal in 1919. At that time, the newspaper named Ada Stafford as the school's only teacher. In 1934, White's Chapel School was one of 27 county schools to offer adult night classes. A new 4-room addition was built onto the school in 1951. In 1952, the following teachers served at the school: Irene Covington, O. Hayes, Elizabeth Jones, and Sarah Snow, with Monroe Jackson as principal. An article from the Memphis Press-Scimitar in 1952 stated that the school had electric lights and an outdoor well. The school also had outdoor toilets, coal-burning heaters in classrooms, and no cafeteria. In 1953, the building pictured above was built. The school was nearly closed in the early 1970's as part of the district's plan to desegregate schools. White's Chapel remained open, and Weaver Elementary was closed in its place. White's Chapel School closed in 2013 but served as a public charter school until 2017. The building was demolished in 2019. The photograph above was taken in the 2000's. (Courtesy of a private collection)

Pictured left is Monroe Melvin Jackson, who served as the principal of White's Chapel School from 1949 to 1965. Professor Jackson served as a Staff Sergeant in the United States Army during WWII from 1942 to 1945. He was also a deacon and trustee at Middle Baptist Church in Whitehaven, TN. (Courtesy of a private collection)

Rev. Joseph S. Simmons served as principal of White's Chapel School from 1970 to 1984. He began his career in education as a fifth-grade teacher at Geeter School in Memphis. Before his time teaching, Simmons served in the United States Army during WWII from 1942 to 1946. He then returned to Memphis and enrolled at Geeter High School. Rev. Simmons went on to attend Tennessee A & I State College, where he graduated in 1950 with a Bachelor of Science in Agriculture. Before being appointed the principal of White's Chapel, Simmons served as the principal of Arlington Elementary, Neshoba Junior High, and Capleville High School. He was a member of Phi Beta Sigma Fraternity, Inc. (Courtesy of a private collection)

# LINCOLN ELEMENTARY SCHOOL

Lincoln Elementary opened in 1922 at 1566 S. Orleans St. in Memphis. According to the Commercial Appeal Newspaper, plans to build two schools for the African American community were finalized in 1922. Those two schools were Porter and Lincoln Schools. Both schools cost approximately $120,000 to build. Both buildings were originally built with eight rooms and were constructed to allow for additions without disrupting classes. One of the earliest principals of Lincoln Elementary was Myrtle Lee Jones. The Commercial Appeal lists her as the principal beginning in 1924, but her tenure could have begun earlier. Before being appointed to Lincoln, Mrs. Jones served as the principal of Morning View School in 1921. In 1926, the faculty of Lincoln Elementary consisted of the following teachers: Myrtle Lee Jones, principal; Oceola Alexander, Etta Drake, Laura E. Harris, Estelle Howell, Zenora Johnson, Lilly D. Pierce, Frances A. Reems, Marie E. Rogers, Mary Wallace, Valerya H. Wallace, and John L. Williams. According to the Commercial Appeal, the 1936 Lincoln faculty consisted of Principal Myrtle L. Jones, Osceola Alexander, Alfred F. Bell, Etta Drake, Laura E. Harris, Estelle Howell, Lilly D. Pierce, Morlean Raynor, Marie E. Rogers, Mary J. Wallace, and Oscar Woolfolk. Lincoln Elementary closed in 2015. Pictured above is a photograph of Lincoln Elementary in the 2000s. (Courtesy of a private collection)

Emmitt L. Washburn, pictured left, served as the principal of Lincoln Elementary School from 1947 to 1961. Born in Gloster, Mississippi, Professor Washburn attended Harper Baptist College in Gloster and graduated from Natchez College in Natchez, MS. After graduating, he served as the East Carroll Normal and Industrial Institute principal in Lake Providence, LA. He arrived in Memphis in 1927 and began teaching at Booker T. Washington High School. In addition to serving as principal of Lincoln Elementary, Washburn also served as the president of the Memphis Youth Services Council. Principal Washburn was also a member of the Sigma Pi Phi Fraternity. (Courtesy of a private collection)

# BROOKS AVENUE SCHOOL
# (ROSENWALD)

The Brooks Avenue School was located on Brooks Avenue in Southwest Memphis. The map image below shows that the school stood east of Highway 61 (S. Third Street). The first Brooks Avenue School dates to 1891. In 1909, Reverend Simon Peter Morris was the principal-teacher at the Brooks School. According to Shelby County School records, Ida Ford was the principal in 1924, and Ethel Sarah Morris and Dora Whitworth served as the school's other teachers. According to the Memphis Press-Scimitar Newspaper, Brooks Avenue School was a 3-room structure with no running water, electricity, cafeteria, or indoor toilets. When the school closed in 1958, the school was consolidated with Geeter School. In 1952, three teachers taught at Brooks Avenue School: Lillie Mae Walker, teacher/principal, Claribelle Howard Weaver, and Bertha Flowers Johnson.

Mrs. Claribelle Howard Weaver served as a teacher at Brooks Avenue in the early 1950s. Born in Memphis, she earned a Bachelor of Arts degree from LeMoyne College in 1943 and a Master of Education degree from Memphis State University in 1975. Mrs. Weaver taught at Brooks Avenue, Collierville, and Weaver Elementary Schools and was the librarian at Mitchell High and South Side High Schools. While a student at LeMoyne College in 1940, she became a member of Alpha Kappa Alpha Sorority, Inc., Beta Tau Chapter. Her husband, Alonzo Weaver, also an educator, served as the first principal of Mitchell High School.

The Brooks Avenue School merged with Geeter High School in 1959. The photograph of the school above was taken in the early 1930s. (Courtesy of a private collection)

Mrs. Lillie Mae Walker, pictured left, served as the principal of the Brooks Avenue School until its closing in 1958. A 1947 graduate of LeMoyne College, Mrs. Walker also earned a Master of Science in Educational Administration from Tennessee State University in 1959. Mrs. Walker taught one year at Mitchell Junior High School in Memphis before being named the principal at Lakeview School in 1959. She would serve as the principal of Lakeview Elementary until retiring in 1972. (Courtesy of the Tennessee State University Special Collection)

# RIVERVIEW SCHOOL

The first Riverview School was located at 260 Joubert Avenue in Southwest Memphis. The school, built to serve the Riverview and Fordhurst Subdivisions, opened in 1952. The Commercial Appeal's description of the school indicates that there were 14 classrooms, toilets in each first and second-grade classroom, a cafetorium with a capacity of 500, a clinic, and a teachers' lounge. This new building was nearly identical to the new Dunn Elementary School built in 1952. The Commercial Appeal named the following teachers as members of the Riverview School Faculty when it opened in 1952: Principal Emma L. Crittenden, Hattie Mae Bond, Elnora Currie, Miss Tom Ella Adams, Mrs. Ernestine Cunningham, Donald Jackson, Mrs. Aulura Gwin, Mrs. Edna H. Swingler, Mrs. Rosa Lee Spicer, Mrs. Bessie Taylor, Miss Mildred Williams, Mrs. Arneda Martin, and Mrs. Geraldine Harris. A local charter school organization currently operates the old elementary school building. (Courtesy of the Tennessee State University Special Collection)

Pictured left is Riverview Elementary School Principal, Miss Emma L. Crittenden. Principal Crittenden began her career as an educator around 1910. Before her tenure at Riverview, she served as the principal of the Florida Street School for 18 years. She was appointed the principal of Riverview School in 1952 and remained there until her retirement in 1956. Mrs. Eleanor Oglesby was appointed principal following Miss Crittenden's retirement. (Courtesy of the Tennessee State University Special Collection)

# KANSAS STREET SCHOOL

The Kansas Street School was built in 1950 to replace the old Virginia Avenue School. The Virginia Street School at Fort Pickering was closed in 1949 to make room for the Frisco and Harrahan Bridges that would cross the Mississippi River. Construction on the new Kansas Street School began in the Fall of 1949. The Kansas Street School, located at 1353 Kansas St., was modern. District leaders touted the school as an example of the type of school African American children in Memphis had access to. In 1959, the Memphis City School Board approved the building of 10 additional classrooms and a special room. 1959 was also the last for Principal Velia J. Wiggins, replaced by Abner B. Owen, Jr. Kansas Elementary merged with Florida Elementary in 1999. The new school was named Florida-Kansas Elementary School. (Courtesy of the Tennessee State University Special Collection)

Velia Jones Wiggins, pictured left, was named the principal of Virginia Avenue School in 1946 when Mattie Currin retired. When Virginia Avenue School closed, she was named principal of the new Kansas Street School. Before being named principal, she was an 8th-grade teacher at Porter Junior High School. Principal Wiggins was a 1938 LeMoyne College graduate with a Bachelor of Science degree and a 1955 graduate of Tennessee State University with a Master of Science in Secondary Education. She was a member of Sigma Gamma Rho Sorority, Inc. and a member of the Bluff City Principals' Association. When Mrs. Wiggins retired, Abner B. Owen, Jr. was appointed principal, where he remained until 1959. (Courtesy of a private collection)

Dr. William H. Sweet was appointed principal of Kansas Street School in 1959. Dr. Sweet was a 1944 graduate of Booker T. Washington High School. After high school, he earned a Bachelor of Science degree in 1949 and a Master of Science degree in 1958, both from Tennessee A & I State College. In 1972, Sweet earned a Doctor in Education degree from the University of Tennessee at Knoxville. Before starting his career in education, he served as an enlisted member of the United States Army and Navy. His first teaching assignment was in 1949 at Melrose High School, where Sweet served as a teacher and coach. Dr. Sweet served Memphis City Schools for 37 years and rose to the position of South Area Superintendent when he retired from the school district in 1986. The school district's Dr. William H. Sweet Academic Award was named in his honor. Dr. Sweet was a member of Omega Psi Phi Fraternity, Inc. (Courtesy of a private collection)

# WEAVER ELEMENTARY SCHOOL
# (ROSENWALD)

Weaver Elementary School was first mentioned in the Memphis newspaper, Commercial Appeal, in 1909. That year, Beulah Moss was the principal of Weaver Elementary. Once located on Weaver Road near Eyres Road, the school was a three-teacher school outside the Memphis city limits. Weaver Road and Weaver School were named after the Weaver Family, whose ancestors owned a large cotton plantation in the area. According to 1919 Shelby County Board records, the following teachers were on the faculty of Weaver School: Rev. Simon P. Morris, Sarah Morris, Ophelia Geeter Ford, and Lena Wortch. In 1927, the school petitioned the school board to build an industrial room onto the existing wood-frame building. According to records, Mrs. Ada E. Scott was the principal in 1930. When she retired, Rev. Simon Peter Morris was appointed principal. He remained principal until the mid-1940s when Isaiah Goodrich, Jr. was appointed principal. In 1952, the following teachers made up the faculty of Weaver School: Mrs. Sarah E. Long, Mrs. Macie Boykins, Miss Ivorie Felton, Miss Annie B. Smith, Mrs. Evelyn Snow, Mrs. Ruth Payne, Mrs. June Pender, Mrs. Orleans P. Knox, Miss, Evelyn Coleman, Miss Florida Jones, Mr. Alonzo Weaver, Mr. Leonard Holley, and Mrs. Elmertha Butler.

Alonzo Weaver was once a teacher and principal at Weaver Elementary School. In 1957, he was named Principal of Mitchell High School. He served as the principal of Mitchell until his retirement in 1979. Mr. Weaver earned a Bachelor of Science degree from LeMoyne College in 1942 and earned a Master of Science degree in Administration and Supervision from Tennessee State University in 1962. He was a member of Alpha Phi Alpha Fraternity, Inc.

In 1973, a judge ordered Weaver School to close as part of a plan to desegregate schools in the area.

Pictured left is Principal Isaiah Goodrich, Jr. He was appointed principal of Weaver School in 1945 when Principal Rev. Simon P. Morris passed away. Professor Goodrich was a high school graduate of Booker T. Washington High School, LeMoyne College, where he earned a Bachelor of Arts degree in 1938, and Memphis State University, where he earned a Master of Arts degree in 1967. Principal Goodrich taught at Geeter High School for two years before beginning his tenure at Weaver School. In 1954, he was appointed principal of the new Ford Road Elementary School. He was a member of Omega Psi Phi Fraternity, Inc. (Courtesy of a private collection)

Torris Jacob "T.J." Toney was the principal of Weaver Elementary from 1957 to 1959. Mr. Toney began his career as a teacher at Woodstock High School. In 1959, he was appointed the assistant principal of Geeter High School. He earned a bachelor's degree from LeMoyne College and a master's from the Tuskegee Institute in 1960. A member of Alpha Phi Alpha Fraternity, Inc., Mr. Toney retired from Memphis City Schools in 1972. (Courtesy of a private collection)

# FLORIDA STREET SCHOOL

The Florida Street School was first mentioned in a Commercial Appeal in 1917, with Thomas L. Stroud listed as the school's acting principal and Mr. John H. Grant as the school's former principal. In 1919, the following teachers made up the faculty at the school: Mattie E. Currin, Principal; Mattie Link, Addie Tanlery, Maggie Radcliff, Viola Overton, Estelle Campbell, Callie Mathis, Mabel Crump, Sallie Cummings, Etta Drake. Construction on the school's new addition began in 1923. The brick, twelve-room structure was three stories tall and was added to the existing wood-frame building that made up the Florida Street School. An architect's drawing of the proposed building is below. In 1934, Emma Crittenden was appointed the school's principal.

By 1936, the school's faculty had more than doubled, growing from ten teachers to twenty-six. That year, the following teachers, including the principal, made up the faculty: Dicie Anderson, Sadie Cleaves, Leonia Dortch, Loveday Fletcher, Barnetta Goldsby, Ruth Hilliard, Lillian Horne, Aubrie Johnson, Emma Johnson, Emma E. Jones, Ruth E. Lane, Ben Lewis, Jr., Mary L. Moore, Eleanor Murdock, Louise Pope, Maggie B. Ratcliffe, Eddie O. Rodgers, Isabelle A. Roulhac, Hattie Saunders, Daisy Stevens, Carlotta Stewart, Beatrice Thompson, Hazel Thompson, Addie Williams, and Alberta Winston.

In 1952, former Grant and Lester School Principal Spencer M. Smith was appointed the school's principal when Miss Crittenden was appointed the new Riverview School principal. When Principal Smith retired in 1962, Callie L. Stevens was appointed the school's new principal.

Callie Lentz Stevens served as the principal of Florida Street School from 1962 to 1970. She was a 1947 graduate of Tennessee A & I State College where she earned a Bachelor of Science in Business Education. She also earned a Master of Art Degree from Northwestern University. She began her teaching career in Missouri and taught at Booker T. Washington High School during the 1950's before her appointment as principal of Melrose Elementary in 1960. In 1962, she was appointed principal of Florida Street Elementary, and she remained there until 1970 when she was named the Southwest Area Assistant Superintendent. She went on to serve as the Memphis City School District's Assistant Superintendent of Curriculum and Instruction before retiring from the school district in 1987. She was member of Alpha Kappa Alpha Sorority, Inc.

Florida Street Elementary closed in 2015 after nearly a century of serving Memphis children.

Thomas L. Stroud served as Florida Street School's acting principal in 1917. He earned a degree in building and contracting from Oklahoma Colored Agricultural and Normal University (Langston University) in Langston, Oklahoma. Stroud taught contracting at the Howe Institute, Kortrecht High School, and Manassas High School for many years. After he retired from teaching, he devoted his time to his work as a contractor and builder. His wife, Josie S. Stroud, taught at the Shelby County Training School. (Woodstock High School). (Courtesy of the Tennessee State University Special Collection)

# HAMNER-TAYLOR SCHOOL
# (ROSENWALD)

The Hamner-Taylor School was a three-room, wood-frame building established around 1909 at the present-day intersection of Winchester Road and Airways Boulevard, just a few blocks from the Memphis International Airport. This image from a 1938 map shows the school's location in a mostly rural area. The school's first principal is believed to have been Callie Earthman. According to the Commercial Appeal, the following teachers made up the faculty of the school: Callie Earthman, Reggie Bryant, Edna Plunkett, and Sherwood Rutherford. In 1924, Callie Earthman, Mattie Robinson, Effie Washington, Theodora Robinson, and Ada Henderson made up the school's faculty. In 1952, Mrs. Ethel Dunn served as the school's principal, and Mrs. Daisy Blackburn and Mrs. Pearl Elmore were the school's teachers. The Memphis Press-Scimitar Newspaper indicated in an article that year that the school lacked running water and a cafeteria, so the children ate cold lunches. However, a concrete walkway at the school's entrance was laid by Geeter High Principal Joseph W. Falls. The Hamner-Taylor School was closed in 1957, and the building was demolished for an Admiral Benbow Hotel.

Callie L. Earthman is believed to be the first principal of the Hamner-Taylor School. According to the Commercial Appeal Newspaper, Mrs. Earthman served as a teacher at John's Chapel School in 1907 before serving as the principal/teacher of Hamner-Taylor. Mrs. Earthman died in 1964 at the age of 87. (Courtesy of the Hill Family, descendants of Callie Earthman).

# DUNN ELEMENTARY SCHOOL

Dunn Elementary opened on Dunn Avenue near Cincinnati Road in 1952. The building was a one-story structure with 14 classrooms and a cafetorium that served grades 1 through 6. When the school opened, it relieved overcrowding at the Cane Creek school on Menager Rd. Mrs. Dovie R. Burnley was the school's first principal. She previously served as the principal of the St. Stephens School in the Berclair Community, which closed in 1952. When St. Stephens closed, Principal Burnley and teachers Mrs. Verneta Riley and Mrs. Mary D. Rook were transferred to the new Dunn School. The other teachers that made up the school's faculty in 1952 were Mrs. Margaret T. Brown, Miss Carrie Watson, Mrs. Beatrice Donoho, Miss Y. Marie Taylor, Mrs. Louise Hines, Miss Fairy M. Peyton, Miss Dorothy L. Akines, and Miss Utoka Quarles. In 1958, eight additional classrooms were added to the school building. Dunn Elementary closed in 2005, and its students were transferred to Norris Elementary School. The photograph above is of Dunn Elementary in 1952. The photograph below is of the faculty of Dunn Elementary in the same year. (Courtesy of the Tennessee State University Special Collection.

Dovie Rogers Burnley was the first principal of the new Dunn Elementary when it opened in 1952. Mrs. Burnley served at Dunn for 25 years. She was a 1947 graduate of LeMoyne College, earning a Bachelor of Arts Degree. Before her time at Dunn Elementary, Mrs. Burnley served as a teacher at city and county schools for more than ten years, and as the principal of St. Stephen School in Berclair until its closing in 1952. Mrs. Burnley was a member of Zeta Phi Beta Sorority, Inc. (Courtesy of a private collection)

# ALONZO LOCKE ELEMENTARY SCHOOL

Alonzo Locke Elementary School dates to 1890, when it was named the St. Paul School. From 1890 to 1947, it was a school for white children in the surrounding area. Located at 688 St. Paul, St. Paul became a school for African American children in September 1947. It was renamed Alonzo Locke Elementary School after famed Peabody Hotel Head Waiter Walter Alonzo Locke, who died in August 1947. The white children of the community were given the choice to transfer to Bruce, Peabody, Riverside, or Christine Schools. The new Alonzo Locke Elementary enrollment was for students transferred from Porter and Leath Schools. The school's new principal was Mrs. Mary E. Murphy. The former principal and teacher of Magnolia Elementary, Mrs. Murphy, attended the Howe Institute, LeMoyne College, Tuskegee Institute, and Tennessee A & I State College. According to the Commercial Appeal, the following teachers made up the faculty of Locke in 1952: Mrs. Annie S. Collins, Mrs. Bertha B. Dillard, Mrs. Helen M. Hayes, Mrs. Jessie R. Hilliard, Mrs. Lillie B. Jeffrey, Miss Willie Lewis, Mrs. Milda M. Nabors, Mrs. Mrtyle Nesbitt, Mr. Abner Owen, Mrs. Alberta B. Sample, Mrs. Vera B. Stevenson, Mrs. Clara Thompkins, Mrs. Zana R. Ward, and Miss Mattie Wilson. When Principal Murphy retired in 1957, she had served as a teacher in Memphis and Shelby County for 39 years. Mrs. Murphy was replaced as principal by Mrs. Hazelle Overton Lewis. (Courtesy of a private collection)

Upon Mrs. Lewis's retirement in 1970, Dr. Reginald L. Green was appointed principal. Dr. Green graduated from Tennessee State University with a Bachelor of Science in Sociology in 1962 and a graduate of Memphis State University with a Master of Education degree in Educational Administration and Supervision in 1967. In 1975, he earned a Doctor of Education in Administration and Supervision from the University of Missouri, Columbia. He began his career in education as a teacher at Lincoln Jr. High School, where he served from 1962 to 1968. In 1969, he was named assistant principal of Manassas High School. In addition to his work with Memphis City Schools, Dr. Green has served as professor, assistant superintendent, deputy superintendent, and superintendent for various colleges and school districts in the United States. A member of Omega Psi Phi Fraternity, Inc., Dr. Green still supports school leaders today.

Locke Elementary remained active for many more decades before closing in 2005. The school's teachers and students were transferred to nearby Georgia Avenue Elementary, and the building was demolished several years later.

Alonzo Locke Elementary School was named after Walter Alonzo Locke, who is pictured left. Mr. Locke served as the head waiter of the Peabody Hotel from 1925 until his passing in 1947. He was born in Trenton, TN, and served as the head waiter of the Hotel Gayoso and Chisca Hotel before the opening of the Peabody. He was known around the country for his ability to remember the names and faces of his guests and his gift for being able to serve without being servile. (Courtesy of the Memphis Public Library & Information Center)

Mrs. Hazelle Overton Lewis, pictured left, served as the principal of Alonzo Locke Elementary from 1957 until her retirement in 1970. She began teaching in Memphis Public Schools in 1919. Principal Lewis graduated from Kortrecht High School, LeMoyne College, Rust College, and Columbia University, earning a Master of Arts in Administration. Before being appointed to Locke Elementary, Mrs. Lewis served as a teacher at LaRose Elementary and Melrose High School. When she retired in 1970, she had spent over 50 years educating the children in the communities surrounding LaRose Elementary, Melrose High, and Alonzo Locke Elementary. (Courtesy of a private collection)

# LEATH ELEMENTARY SCHOOL

Leath Elementary began in the 1870s as a grammar school for white children of the area surrounding the school at Linden and Wellington. In 1940, the school was converted to an all-black school. Leath School was named after former Memphis Public Schools Superintendent James T. Leath, the son of Sarah Leath, the founder of Memphis's first orphanage. When the school year opened in September of 1940, nearly 1,000 students had enrolled. Later that year, the school's kitchen and playground were expanded, and two additional teachers were added. The first principal of the new Leath School was Mrs. Leslie H. Taylor. She served as the principal of the school from 1940 to 1954. She became a principal when she was appointed to Grant School in 1934. According to the Commercial Appeal, the following teachers made up the faculty of the school: Leslie Taylor, principal; Theresa Barksdale, Mary Bradford, Catherine Branch, Annette Brown, Estelle Campbell, Elaine Douglas, Inez Dunn, Sarah E. Davis, Jessie Gwyn, Julie Hanell, Lula Hurd, Lillian Maxey, Buncye Moore, Emmett L. Rice, Anna L. Rogers, Jeannette Smith, Helen White, Sadie Williams, Jessie Woodfin, Clara Perkins, Annie Mae Richardson, Delia Partee, and Ida Peary. When Principal Taylor retired in 1954, Miss Charlsye M. Heard was appointed principal. Mrs. Taylor and Miss Heard were members of Sigma Gamma Rho Sorority, Inc. Leath Elementary closed in 1982. Pictured above is the Leath School in the early 1970's. (Courtesy of the Memphis Public Library & Information Center)

Pictured left is Mrs. Leslie H. Pope Taylor. She served as the first principal of the new Leath School from 1940 to 1954. Mrs. Taylor was a 1933 graduate of LeMoyne College, earning a Bachelor of Arts Degree in Education. She was elected a teacher at Grant School following her graduation in 1933. The following year, she was appointed principal of Grant. Mrs. Taylor, a member of Sigma Gamma Rho Sorority, Inc., retired from Memphis City Schools in 1954. (Courtesy of the Tennessee State University Special Collection)

Charlsye Heard served as the principal of Leath School from 1954 to 1971. Miss Heard graduated from Rust College in Holly Springs, MS. Previously, she served as a teacher at Hyde Park Elementary School. Miss Heard, a member of Sigma Gamma Rho Sorority, Inc., retired in 1971. (Courtesy of the Tennessee State University Special Collection)

# PARK AVENUE SCHOOL

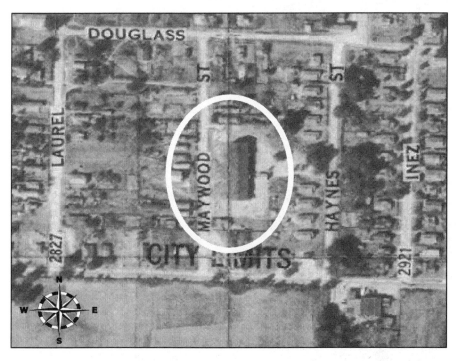

The Park Avenue School was a 10-room school building on Maywood Street and Park Avenue in Orange Mound. The image above of a 1939 map shows the school bordered by Park Avenue to the South, Douglass to the North, and Haynes to the East. Additionally, the school was located just inside of the Memphis city limits. The school first opened in 1924 with nine teachers. Community leader and Baptist Minister Dr. Sutton Elbert Griggs spoke for the special occasion at the school's grand opening. Rev. Henry L. Peterson served as the school's first principal. According to the Commercial Appeal Newspaper, the school was painted and received other repairs by the school district in 1933. In 1936, the following teachers and assistants made up the faculty at Park Avenue School: Susie J. Crawford (principal), Maggie Donelson, Callie Earthman, Ida Y. Ford, Ophelia Hawkins, Willa Mae Hurd, Gertrude Johnson, Lois King, Lucille Randall, Gladys Sharp, Agnes P. Taylor, and Jessie Bond. In 1938, Mr. Ernest C. Ball, Superintendent of Memphis City Schools, consolidated Park Avenue School and Melrose High School.

Pictured left is Rev. Henry L. Peterson. Rev. Peterson was the first principal of Park Avenue School. He also served as the pastor of Bethel Presbyterian Church in Memphis from its founding in 1911 until 1933. In 1919, he was the principal of Millington Junior High School (E.A. Harrold). (Courtesy of the Tennessee State University Special Collection)

# FORD ROAD ELEMENTARY SCHOOL

Ford Road Elementary School opened in Southwest Memphis in 1954. Serving the Walker Homes Community, the school was a one-story building with twelve classrooms and a cafetorium on Ford and Mitchell Roads. The first principal of Ford Road School was Mr. Isaiah Goodrich, Jr., who previously served as principal of nearby Weaver Elementary. In 1955, a 16-room addition to the school was completed, which brought the total number of classrooms to twenty-eight. Just before Thanksgiving in 1960, a fire severely damaged one of the three buildings on campus. The damaged building contained classrooms and the school's cafeteria. The displaced students were temporarily moved to Walker Elementary and Mitchell Road High School. Principal Isaiah Goodrich, Jr. retired as principal of Ford Road Elementary in 1975. The school remains active within the Memphis Shelby County School District.

Pictured left is Principal Isaiah Goodrich, Jr., in the early 1950's. He was appointed the first principal of Ford Road School in 1954. Professor Goodrich was a high school graduate of Booker T. Washington High School, LeMoyne College, where he earned a Bachelor of Arts in 1938, and Memphis State University, where he earned a Master of Arts Degree in 1967. Principal Goodrich taught at Geeter High School for two years before beginning his tenure at Weaver School. In 1954, he was appointed principal of the new Ford Road Elementary School. He was a member of Omega Psi Phi Fraternity, Inc. (Courtesy of the Tennessee State University Special Collection)

# Chapter Three

# Schools in Northwest Shelby County (Uptown, New Chicago, Binghampton, Frayser, Raleigh, and Millington)

## WOODSTOCK HIGH SCHOOL (ROSENWALD)

Woodstock High School began as the Shelby County Training School (S.C.T.S.) for African American students in 1911 in the Woodstock community, outside the Memphis city limits in North Shelby County. Thomas J. Johnson served as the first principal of the school. Pictured above is one of the main buildings on the Shelby County Training School campus in the early 1920s. (Courtesy of the University of Virginia Collection). The photograph below is of the new building in the 1940s. (Courtesy of the Tennessee State University Special Collection)

Like many rural schools of the day, students lived at the school or were boarders. These students performed many daily chores, such as laundering, gardening, cooking, and cleaning. At the school, the boys were responsible for planting and tending gardens and fields, which were the source of food for students and faculty members who all lived on the property. The girls were often responsible for cooking and sewing. In addition to many domestic and industrial tasks, students had a rigorous academic course load to manage. The close-knit atmosphere experienced by teachers and students created a link of caring and concern that extended long past regular school hours. The school became a high school in 1913. In 1923, the S.C.T.S. graduated its first high school class. Three students received their diplomas that year. The school's name was officially changed to Woodstock High School in 1963. African American students from elementary schools within a 30-mile radius of Woodstock were bused to Woodstock to finish their high school education. Because of the dormitories on campus, boys and girls from as far away as Arkansas would attend Woodstock High School. (Courtesy of the University of Virginia Collection)

In 1970, efforts to desegregate schools forced Woodstock's students to attend Millington Central High School. The school became an elementary school with Principal John Strong serving as principal. It now serves middle school students in North Shelby County. The Teachers' Home at Woodstock in 1915 is pictured above. The picture below shows male students and teachers outside of the school's workshop in 1915. (Courtesy of the University of Virginia Collection)

Pictured right is Thomas J. Johnson, who served as the first principal of the Shelby County Training School. Professor Johnson was a graduate of Alcorn A&M College in Mississippi. In 1913, he established the Shelby County Training School at Woodstock, TN. He was the principal until 1927, when he became the principal of Klondike Elementary School in Memphis, TN. He would remain the principal of Klondike until his retirement in 1949. (Courtesy of the Tennessee State University Special Collection)

Pictured right is Principal Roy Jacob Roddy. He began teaching at the Shelby County Training School (S.C.T.S.) in 1920. Roddy became the second principal in the history of the SCTC when T.J. Johnson left the school in 1927. He remained the principal until his retirement in 1966. He received a Bachelor of Science degree in 1946 and a Master of Science degree in 1960 from Tennessee State University. (Courtesy of the Tennessee State University Special Collection)

Mr. John E. Strong, Jr., pictured left, served as the principal of Woodstock School from 1966 to 1989. Principal Strong is a 1948 graduate of Barret's Chapel High School and a 1952 graduate of Lane College in Jackson, TN. He began his career in education in 1952 as a teacher at Brunswick Jr. High School in Shelby County. Later that year, he served in the United States Army during the Korean War until 1956. He would serve in the U.S. Army until 1956. Upon returning, he was hired as a teacher at Geeter High School by Dr. Joseph W. Falls. In 1960, he was appointed principal of Eads Elementary School in Eads, TN. In 1962, he was appointed principal of Weaver School, where he remained until 1965. He was appointed the principal of Capleville High School near the end of the 1964-1965 school year. Mr. Strong served as the principal of Capleville High until 1966 when he was named the principal of Woodstock High School. He served as the principal for 23 years, ultimately retiring in 1989. Mr. Strong is an active member of Alpha Phi Alpha Fraternity, Inc. (Courtesy of the collection of Rev. Dr. Clennon Saulsberry, Sr.).

Imogene Usher Hill was a music teacher and assistant principal at Woodstock High School. A talented singer, Mrs. Hill was a 1936 graduate of Lane College, earning a Bachelor of Arts degree, and a 1964 graduate of Memphis State University with a Master of Arts degree in education. Mrs. Hill began her time at Woodstock High in 1948. She retired in 1982 as a guidance counselor at Millington Central High School after serving the Shelby County School District for 34 years. (Courtesy of a private collection)

# DOUGLASS HIGH SCHOOL

The first known public school established in the historic Douglass Community was the Leawood (Leewood) School. It was established before 1900. Two of the school's first principals were Susie J. Crawford and William M. Coke. This school, located at Brookins and Orr, was renamed Douglass after the Douglass subdivision that the school served. In 1930, records indicate that fifteen teachers and a principal made up the faculty in the wood-frame building. In 1936, a new school building opened to replace the old one destroyed by fire in 1934. Funded by the Works Progress Administration (WPA), created by President F. Roosevelt, this second building served the community's children for eight years. That building is pictured above. In 1953, a new two-story building opened. In addition to rooms for labs, vocational shops, art, and domestic sciences, twelve additional classrooms would allow the school to double its capacity. That building is pictured below. (Courtesy of a private collection)

Since its founding, Douglass High School provided students opportunities to grow in and out of the classroom. Students had opportunities to participate in sports, the arts, and civic activities. Many of its students (including the author's mother) fondly remember their time at Douglass High. In 1981, Douglass High School closed. In 2006, the old Douglass High School building was demolished to make room for a newly constructed school. The new Douglass High School officially opened in 2008, with Douglass High graduate Janet Thompson serving as principal. Below is a group of students with their teacher, Samuel Helm. Mr. Helm served as a teacher at Douglass before serving as the principal of Hyde Park and Shannon Elementary Schools. (Courtesy of a private collection)

Lucky Charles Sharp, pictured left, served as the principal of Douglass School from 1929 to 1952. Before his tenure at Douglass High School, he was a star athlete at Prairie View A&M in Texas. He graduated from LeMoyne College, taught at the Woodstock Training School, and served as the principal of Millington Jr. High before coming to Douglass. Professor Sharp led Douglass through the Great Depression and a disastrous fire that destroyed part of the school. Part of his legacy is the Live at Home Project that he helped establish. The focus of this project was to establish gardens while canning fruits and vegetables for the students and residents of the Douglass Community. (Courtesy of the Tennessee State University Special Collection)

Jesse Dozzell Springer was named principal of Douglass High School in 1952, following the retirement of long-time principal Lucky C. Sharp. A 1926 graduate of Howard University, Springer served as a teacher at Booker T. Washington from 1927 to 1941 and Melrose Jr. High in 1941. Principal Springer was also a graduate of Columbia University's Teachers College. He served in the United States Army during WWII, reaching the rank of Captain. Following his time at Douglass High, he returned to Booker T. Washington as principal in 1959 when Blair T. Hunt retired. Professor Springer retired from Memphis Public Schools in 1970. He was a member of Kappa Alpha Psi Fraternity. (Courtesy of a private collection)

Melvin Nathaniel Conley served as the principal of Douglass High School from 1959 to 1969. He began his tenure with Memphis City Schools in 1951 at Florida Elementary School. Before his time in public education, Conley served in the United States Army during WWII and was a director for the Boone-Higgins Trade School on Beale Street in Memphis. This trade school supported African American veterans returning from the war. Before leading Douglass, Conley also served as a teacher at Melrose High, the principal of Hyde Park Elementary from 1956 to 1957, and the principal of Porter Junior High from 1957 to 1959. He completed his tenure with Memphis City Schools by serving as principal of Melrose High School from 1969 to 1979. Melvin N. Conley was a member of Kappa Alpha Psi Fraternity, Inc. (Courtesy of a private collection)

Dr. Omar Robert Robinson, Jr. served as the Douglass High Choral Director from 1950 to 1969. A graduate of Douglass High, he attended Tennessee A & I State College, where he graduated in 1950. Dr. Robinson received a Master of Music from the American Conservatory of Music in Chicago, IL, and a Doctor of Music Education Degree from Western Colorado University. He served as the choral director at Langston University before returning to Memphis to head the Division of Arts and Letters at Shelby State Community College. Omar Robinson Blvd in the Douglass Community is named in his honor. Dr. Robinson was a member of Phi Beta Sigma Fraternity, Inc. (Courtesy of a private collection)

John Edward Wesley is another educator who began his career as a teacher at Douglass High School in 1951. A Tennessee A & I State College graduate, he earned a Bachelor of Science in Biology in 1951 and a Master of Science in Educational Administration and Supervision in 1960. After serving in the United States Army as a Medic during the Korean War, he was appointed to Lester High School in 1955 and served as a teacher, coach, athletic director, and assistant principal. In 1969, he was named principal following the retirement of Robert M. Morris. He remained the principal of Lester High until he was appointed principal of East High School in 1972, He also served as the principal of Douglass High from 1976 to 1981 and Northside High School from 1981 until his retirement in 1986.

Daniel Ward began his career in education in 1959 as a teacher at Douglass High School. He graduated from Booker T. Washington High School and Tennessee State University, earning a Bachelor of Science in 1956 and a Master of Science in Secondary School Instruction in 1960. In 1956, Ward joined the United States Air Force Pilot Program. From 1956 to 1984, Lt. Col. Ward served in the U.S. Air Force and Air National Guard, with most of that time being served as a pilot. Mayor Henry Loeb appointed him to the Memphis Airport Authority in 1967. Ward served as the assistant principal of Hyde Park Elementary and the principal of Grant, Porter Jr. High, Orleans, Vance Jr. High, and Fairley High before being named assistant superintendent of secondary schools. Mr. Ward served as the interim superintendent of Memphis City Schools from 2007 to 2008. He is a member of Omega Psi Phi Fraternity, Inc.

# MANASSAS HIGH SCHOOL (ROSENWALD)

Manassas School was established in 1899. The original Manassas building was a two--room frame structure outside the city limits on the east side of Manassas Street, just south of current-day Firestone Avenue. William H. Foote was appointed as its first principal. The small two-room structure would double its capacity when two more rooms were added in 1902. In 1905, Principal Foote resigned, and Josephine Sims was named principal. She served three years in that capacity, and Rose Washington was named principal in 1908. During that time, Laura O. Johnson and Ella Mosely were teachers at the school. Pictured above is the school's auditorium. (Courtesy of a private collection) It would later be named after former principal Cora P. Taylor. It was demolished in 1976. The second school building, constructed in 1918, is in the background. Below is a photo of Manassas with new and old buildings present. (Courtesy of University of Memphis Special Collection)

Cora P. Taylor was appointed the principal of Manassas in 1909. The previous year, the Commercial Appeal listed her as the teacher at the Raleigh Colored School. Part of her legacy is the growth that Manassas experienced under her leadership. She partnered with community leaders to purchase land that would be the site of the new sixteen-room school building completed in 1918. In 1927, an auditorium, named in her honor, was built on campus with bricks that Principal Taylor transported from nearby Millington. When she became too ill to maintain her duties as principal, J. Ashton Hayes was named principal in 1929. (Courtesy of the Tennessee State University Special Collection)

James Ashton Hayes was appointed the new principal of Manassas in 1929. A graduate of Lane College, he taught in Henning, Tennessee, Ripley, TN, at the Hopkinsville Colored School in Hopkinsville, KY, and he coached football at Tennessee A & I State College in Nashville, Tennessee. Hayes also coached at Booker T. Washington High before going to Manassas. For the next 23 years, he would lead Manassas High. In 1938, a new Manassas building opened to replace the old 16-room structure. A new addition containing a library, a cafeteria, and two science rooms was added in 1953. When it became a requirement that all Memphis principals have a master's degree, Hayes, with two years remaining until his retirement, stepped aside for Louis B. Hobson of Lester School to become the principal of Manassas. J.A. Hayes spent 1953 to 1955 as the principal of Lester School. (Courtesy of the Tennessee State University Special Collection)

Louis Burton Hobson served as the principal of Manassas from 1953 to 1974. Before leading Manassas, Professor Hobson served as the principal of Lester Elementary from 1949-1953. Before that, he served as a social science teacher at Manassas. A graduate of Virginia Union University, Western Reserve University, and the University of Michigan, Hobson served in the United States Army during WWII, reaching the rank of Staff Sergeant. Many of his former students remember him for uplifting leadership. He often told his students they could do and be whatever they wanted. Because of this belief, Manassas graduates have contributed to Memphis and beyond. Mr. Burton retired in 1974. He was a member of Phi Beta Sigma Fraternity, Inc. (Courtesy of a private collection)

Addie Dandridge Jones was a long-time educator at Manassas High. Mrs. Jones began her 42-year career at Manassas as the secretary to the principal. She served as a history teacher and, lastly, the head guidance counselor at the time of her retirement in 1971. Jones earned a Bachelor of Arts degree from LeMoyne College in 1936 and a Master of Science in Guidance and Counseling in 1968 from Tennessee State University. In 1973, she authored the book, *Portrait of a Ghetto School*, which tells the history of Manassas High School. She was a member of Delta Sigma Theta Sorority and the Memphis Links, Inc. (Courtesy of a private collection)

Elihu Alonzo "E.A." Teague began his career in education by serving as the teaching principal at the Baptist Industrial College in DeSoto County, MS, where his father, Rev. Alexander L. Teague, was one of the school's founders. He served at the school for two years before becoming the principal of Eads Junior High School. Teague led Eads School from around 1915 until 1925 when he was elected a teacher at Manassas High School. He retired in 1959 after 34 years of service to the students and faculty of Manassas High School. (Courtesy of a private collection)

Rochester Neely, Sr., pictured left, was an assistant principal at Manassas High School under the leadership of Principal Louis B. Hobson. He was a graduate of the Woodstock Training School in Millington, TN. After graduation, Neely attended LeMoyne College, where he graduated in 1939 with a Bachelor of Arts degree. After graduating from LeMoyne, Neely taught briefly before serving in the United States Army during WWII, where he earned the rank of 1st Sergeant. When he returned from service, he was hired as a teacher at Grant School in 1946. In 1962, he was named an assistant principal of Manassas High School. Mr. Neely earned a Master of Arts from Memphis State University in 1964. In 1969, he was appointed principal of Vollentine Elementary School, where he remained until his retirement in 1980. He was a member of Omega Psi Phi Fraternity, Inc. (Courtesy of a private collection)

# LESTER HIGH SCHOOL

Construction began on the new Lester High School in the Binghampton Community in 1955. The school opened in 1956, with Andrew B. Bland serving as the school's first principal. Mr. Bland previously served as the principal of Hyde Park Elementary School. The school was a three-story building with 14 classrooms, a library, offices, labs, shops, and cafetorium. In 1959, Carpenter Elementary, housed in a wing of Lester High, opened to serve children in grades 1-3. That same year, Andrew Bland left Lester and returned to Hyde Park Elementary. His replacement was Robert H. Morris, the former principal of Grant School. Mr. Morris served as the school's principal until his retirement in 1969. The school's assistant principal, John Wesley, was appointed principal in the summer of 1969.

Court rulings that mandated school desegregation forced the closure of Lester High School as a high school in 1972. Lester students in grades 10-12 were sent to East High, and East High students in grades 7-9 would attend the new Lester Junior High. Students at Carpenter Elementary were sent to East Elementary, while students in grades 4-6 remained at Lester Elementary. The old Lester High School building is a public charter school today. The photograph above is the main entrance of the old Lester High School. (Courtesy of The University of Memphis Special Collection)

Robert Herman Morris served as the principal of Lester High School from 1959 to 1969. Mr. Morris received his early education at the LeMoyne Normal Institute. He earned a Bachelor of Science in Education in 1927 and a Master of Science in Secondary Education in 1956 from Tennessee A & I State College. From 1927 to 1953, Principal Morris taught physics at Booker T. Washington High School. In 1953, he was named the principal of Grant Elementary School. He remained at Grant until 1959. His appointment as Lester High principal in 1959 made him the second principal in the school's history. In 1969, he retired from Memphis City Schools after 42 years of service. He was a member of Alpha Phi Alpha Fraternity, Inc. (Courtesy of a private collection)

John Edward Wesley served as the principal of Lester High School until 1972. After earning a Bachelor of Science in Biology from Tennessee A & I State College in 1951, he began his career in education as a teacher at Douglass High School in 1951. Wesley went on to earn a Master of Science in Educational Administration and Supervision from Tennessee State University in 1960. After serving in the United States Army as a medic during the Korean War in 1955, he was appointed to Lester High School, where he served as a teacher, coach, athletic director, and assistant principal. Wesley remained the principal of Lester High until he was appointed principal of East High School in 1972. He also served as the principal of Douglass High from 1976 to 1981 and Northside High School from 1981 until his retirement in 1986.

# LESTER ELEMENTARY SCHOOL

Lester School was first established as the Scott Avenue School in the Binghamton community, outside the city limits before 1914. The school was located at Scott Avenue and Broad Street. At that time, the school had four teachers and was a wood-frame building. In 1919, the city of Memphis annexed the community, making the school a part of the Memphis Public School District. A new 12-room school building was constructed at 584 Lester in 1924 and renamed Lester School. Mattie E. Smith, principal from 1914 to 1946, and Spencer M. Smith, principal from 1946 to 1949, were two of the school's earliest principals. Pictured above is the Lester School building in the 1930's. (Courtesy of a private collection) Below is a 1944 photograph of the school with its new additions. (Courtesy of the Tennessee State University Special Collection)

Louis Hobson was appointed the principal of Lester Elementary in 1949, and Spencer Smith was named principal of Grant Elementary School. James A. Hayes was named Lester Elementary principal in 1953 after stepping down from the principalship of Manassas High. Louis B. Hobson took his place as Manassas High principal. The photograph above is of a primary grade class at Lester Elementary. Below is a photo of the school's basketball team in the early 1950s. (Courtesy of a private collection)

Mattie Elizabeth Smith, pictured left, was one of the first principals of Lester School. She was appointed principal in 1914 when the school faculty consisted of only four teachers, including the principal. In 1907, she was named a teacher at the Frayser Colored School. She promoted her students' knowledge as they were frequent participants in the city's Tri-State Fair's agriculture exhibits. During her tenure as principal of Lester Elementary, she led the school and community through its annexation into the city of Memphis and expansion of the school campus. She retired in 1946 after 32 years of service to Lester Elementary School. (Courtesy of the Tennessee State University Special Collection)

Spencer M. Smith, pictured right, was Mattie Smith's successor as principal of Lester School. He was appointed to the role of principal in 1946 upon Mrs. Smith's retirement. He began his teaching career as a science teacher at Booker T. Washington High School after graduating from Wilberforce University in 1924. In 1949, he was appointed the principal of Grant School. When he retired in 1962, he was the principal of Florida Elementary School. He was a member of Alpha Phi Alpha Fraternity, Inc. (Courtesy of a private collection)

Theodore R. Johnson served as the principal of Lester Elementary for twenty-three years, from 1960 to 1973. A graduate of LeMoyne College, he earned a Bachelor of Science Degree in 1951. He was appointed to his first teaching position in 1951 at Hyde Park Elementary and was named principal of Kortrecht Elementary in 1959. When Lester Elementary Principal, Mrs. Eddie O. Rodgers, died in 1960, Mr. Johnson was appointed principal. In 1973, he left Lester Elementary to accept the principal appointment at Caldwell Elementary. After 9 years at Caldwell, he was appointed principal of Levi Elementary in 1982. In 1988, he was appointed the principal of Lincoln Elementary and remained at the school until 1994. After over 40 years as an educator in Memphis City Schools, Mr. Johnson retired in 1995. Mr. Johnson was a member of Kappa Alpha Psi Fraternity, Inc.

The original Lester Elementary on Lester Street was demolished in 2009, and in 2017, the remaining portion of the annex building constructed in the 1950s was also demolished.

# E.A. HARROLD JUNIOR HIGH SCHOOL (ROSENWALD)

The history of E.A. Harrold School began when the school was named Millington Jr. High School. It was founded before 1907. One of the school's first principals was George Hegler. According to the Commercial Appeal, Bettie Fields served as a teacher at the school in 1908. A 1909 article from the same newspaper named William Jefferson Millington Jr. High's principal and Flora Mebane, an assistant. In 1923, a new school, built with the assistance of the Rosenwald Fund, was completed. The school was a two-story building that provided space for eight teachers. Over the next few years, rooms were added, wiring was completed, and updates were made to the principal's house. The school's name was changed to E.A. Harrold Jr. High School in July 1952, following approval from the Shelby County School Board. The name change was made for two reasons: 1) to honor the former Shelby County Schools Board Chair E.A. Harrold, who died in 1950, and 2) to eliminate the confusion created by having a Black and a White school both named Millington Jr. High. Pictured above is the school's administration building. The photograph below is the school's auditorium/gym. Both photographs are from the early 1950's. (Courtesy of the Tennessee State University Special Collection)

The Millington Jr. High's principal's home was also on the school grounds. The photograph above captures the principal's residence in the early 1950's. According to records, the faculty of E.A. Harrold School consisted of the following teachers in 1952: Cornell Wells, Principal; Martin Robinson, Jr., Assistant Principal; Charles W. Horner, Assistant Principal; Susie Parks, Lillian Coleman; Dorothy Bond Herring, Vera Bell, Doris V. Stovall, Ida Mae McLeroy, Grace Horner, Hattie Stewart, Valois Perry, Lavelle Fouse, Mabel Jenkins, Ira L. Wells, Bethel Alexander, Estelle Ransom, Bernice Cole Phillips, Vernon T. Jones, James T. Coleman, Mary Wells Johnson, Nadine Moseley, and Ellen Jones. E.A. Harrold School closed permanently in 2021. (Courtesy of the Tennessee State University Special Collection)

E.A. Harrold Jr. High School was named after former Shelby County School Board Chair Elton Andrew Harrold in 1952. Mr. Harrold died in 1950 and was a prominent and influential businessman in Millington, TN. He owned the E.A. Harrold Department Store, which had been open since 1898.

Pictured left is Reverend Henry L. Peterson. Rev. Peterson was one of the first principals of E.A. Harrold Jr. High School. While it is unclear when he was appointed school principal, the Commercial Appeal Newspaper indicates that he was the principal as early as 1919. Rev. Peterson also served as the pastor of Bethel Presbyterian Church in Memphis from its founding in 1911 until 1933. In 1924, the Commercial Appeal Newspaper listed Rev. Peterson as the principal of the Park Avenue School, once located in the Orange Mound Community in Memphis. (Courtesy of the Tennessee State University Special Collection)

Cornell Lawrence Wells served as the principal of E.A. Harrold School from 1938 to 1968. Mr. Wells began his education career at 18 when he was appointed to teach at the Hamner-Taylor School in Southwest Shelby County. The following year, he was appointed principal of the Spring Hill School located near Raleigh, TN. He was 19 years old and the youngest principal in the county. Mr. Wells, a LeMoyne College, and Tennessee State University graduate became the first African American assistant superintendent in the Shelby County School District in 1970. His wife, Ira Wells, was also an educator and served as the principal of Spring Hill School when he accepted a position at the Shelby County School's Central Office. (Courtesy of the Tennessee State University Special Collection)

Pictured is Charles Wesley Horner, former assistant principal of E.A. Harrold School. Mr. Wesley began his time at E.A. Harrold in 1952. He served as one of two assistant principals and a seventh-grade teacher. A 1942 graduate of the Mississippi Industrial College in Holly Springs, MS, Horner served as Staff Sergeant in the United States Air Force during WWII. After his time at E.A. Harrold, he served as principal of Walker Elementary School in Southwest Shelby County. Principal Horner retired in 1984 after serving schools in Shelby County for over 30 years. (Courtesy of the Tennessee State University Special Collection)

# CALDWELL ELEMENTARY SCHOOL

The first known Caldwell School was built at 228 Hickory Avenue in North Memphis around 1913. One of the earliest references to the school in the Commercial Appeal was in 1916 when the newspaper reported on how the Memphis Public School Board discussed where the students in the Bickford Community would go to school after the Caldwell building was destroyed by fire. In 1919, Reverend Thomas Oscar Fuller described Caldwell School as "spacious and well appointed." At that time, 271 students were enrolled with five teachers. Pictured above is Caldwell School around 1922. (Courtesy of The University of Memphis Special Collections)

One of the earliest principals of Caldwell School was Jeanette Shivers. Mrs. Shivers served as the principal of the school from 1913 to 1949. A great organizer, she involved families in the community with growing vegetable gardens and canning the produce for students and patrons. A kindergarten program was first established at the school in 1939. When Principal Shivers retired in 1949, Mrs. Hettie McDaniels was appointed principal. A former teacher at Kortrecht Grammar School, Principal McDaniels served until 1959, when she became the principal of Walker Elementary School in Southwest Memphis, and Miss Frankie Cash was appointed the new principal of Caldwell School. In 1956, the Memphis City School Board approved the construction of a new school building in the community. The existing school was the last remaining wood-frame school building with an outdoor toilet in the city. That new 26-room building at 230 Henry Avenue opened in 1957. Pictured above is Caldwell School in 1922. Pictured below is the Caldwell building constructed in 1957. (Courtesy of a private collection)

Herbert William Robinson, Jr. served as the principal of Caldwell Elementary from 1961 to 1969. Mr. Robinson was a 1944 graduate of Booker T. Washington High School. He also earned a Bachelor of Science degree in History from Tennessee A & I State College in 1950 and a Master of Arts degree in Education from Memphis State University in 1962. His first teaching assignment was at Melrose School in 1950. He also served as the principal of Manassas Elementary beginning in 1959 before being promoted to the role of principal of Caldwell in 1961. In 1969, he was appointed principal of Douglass High School and the principal of East High School in 1976. He was named principal of Memphis Technical High School in 1980. Principal Robinson retired from Memphis City Schools in 1982 after 32 years of service. (Courtesy of a private collection)

# GRANT/POPE ELEMENTARY SCHOOL

According to the Commercial Appeal Newspaper, Grant School opened in September 1885. Grant School was a one-story frame building with six rooms and approximately 200 students at that time. Before being named the Grant School, the school was called the Auction Street School because it was located on Auction Street near Seventh Street. In 1885, Mr. Alexander W. Brown served as the principal, and the following teachers made up the faculty: I.J. Graham, Fannie J. Thompson, Miss Ida B. Wells, Mrs. S.B. Hall, and Miss Tera Owens. Mr. J. Thomas Turner was appointed principal of Grant in 1888 when Principal Brown passed away. Principal L.H. Fields was appointed principal in 1892. He served as the principal until 1915. In 1908, the following teachers made up Grant School's faculty: L.H. Fields, Principal, J.D. Cotton, M.A. Jackson, Mattye E. Porter, Lilly J. Yancey, C. Belle Jackson, S.S. Brown, Myrtie E. Allen, F.L. Cummings, Jessie B. Rudd, Maybelle C. Irving, Georgia A. Anderson, Ethel C. Jones, and Marie B. Jones. A new, two-story brick school building was constructed at 500 N. Seventh near Auction Street in 1913. From 1915 until 1959, Grant School was led by the following principals: J. M. Jones, E.L. Honesty, Daniel W. Gary (1935 -1945), Harry T. Cash (1945-1949), Spencer M. Smith (1949-1952), Richard Thompson (1952-1953), Robert H. Morris (1953-1959), William Cox (1959-1960), Frank J. Lewis (1960-1967), Daniel Ward (1967-1968). Pictured above is Grant School in 1919. (Courtesy of the Memphis Public Library & Information Center)

With the building of the new Dr. H. P. Hurt Village Housing Project for white citizens in 1953, the neighborhood around Grant School began to change. Many white children who attended nearby LeRoy Pope Elementary lived next door to the all-black Grant School. In 1959, the Memphis City School Board decided to have the Grant School switch buildings with the LeRoy Pope School. The teachers and students at both schools would switch buildings and furniture but retain their school's name. Once the move was completed, Grant School was located at 190 Chelsea Avenue. Because of the switch, the school is often called Grant/Pope School or Pope/Grant School. The school was demolished, and the Memphis City School District sold the property to the Memphis Housing Authority in the early 1980s. Pictured above is the old LeRoy Pope Elementary building. (Courtesy of the Memphis Public Library & Information Center)

Robert Herman Morris served as the principal of Grant School from 1953 to 1959. Mr. Morris received his early education at the LeMoyne Normal Institute, where he earned a Bachelor of Science in Education in 1927 and a Master of Science in Secondary Education in 1956 from Tennessee A & I College. From 1927 to 1953, Principal Morris taught physics at Booker T. Washington High School. In 1959, he was named the principal of Lester High School. In 1969, he retired from Memphis City Schools after 42 years of service. (Courtesy of a private collection)

Dr. William W. "Tiny" Cox, pictured right, served as the principal of Grant School from 1958 to 1960. A graduate of Manassas High School, Dr. Cox served in the United States Army during WWII from 1944 to 1946, reaching the rank of Staff Sergeant. Cox earned a Bachelor of Science in Biology in 1950 and a Master of Science in Elementary Education in 1962 at Tennessee A & I University. He began teaching in 1951 at Kansas Elementary. In 1958, he was named principal of Grant School. He was appointed principal of the new Chicago Park Elementary School in 1960. After Chicago Park Elementary was closed, Principal Cox was appointed principal of Kansas Elementary School. Dr. Cox retired from Memphis City Schools in 1989. He was a member of Alpha Phi Alpha Fraternity, Inc. and a 1983 inductee of the Tennessee State University Hall of Fame for his accomplishments in Boxing. (Courtesy of the Tennessee State University Special Collection)

Dr. Frank J. Lewis served as the principal of Grant School from 1960 to 1967. He was a 1950 Tennessee A & I State College graduate, earning a Bachelor of Science Degree in Health and Physical Education. His career in education began in 1950 when he was hired as a teacher at Barret's Chapel High School. He taught biology, health, and physical education. He later coached and taught physical education at Melrose High School. After his time at Grant, he was appointed the principal of AB Hill Elementary and Airways Junior High. He retired after serving as an assistant professor of physical education at Memphis State University. A hall-of-fame basketball player at Tennessee State University, Dr. Lewis was a member of Kappa Alpha Psi Fraternity, Inc. (Courtesy of a private collection)

# KLONDIKE ELEMENTARY SCHOOL

According to the Memphis Avalanche Newspaper, Klondike School opened in October 1900. When the school opened, classes were held in a neighborhood church. The following teachers made up the first faculty of Klondike School: Cora Price Taylor, Floy Cowan, Hattie Foote, Hallie Taylor, and Phillip Dickerson. By 1901, Phillip A. Dickerson was the school's principal, a four-room, wood-frame building with approximately 150 students. In 1909, four additional rooms were added to the existing structure. In 1910, James M. Jones was serving as the principal, and the school grew to a faculty of 10 teachers and 450 students. By 1915, Elijah H. Triplett was the school's principal. From 1927 to 1942, Thomas J. Johnson, former principal of Woodstock High School, served as the principal of Klondike. The following teachers made up the school's faculty in 1936, according to the Commercial Appeal: Thomas J. Johnson, Laura Asamore, Mattie R. Doggett, Mollie Franklin, Emma B. Jones, Bertice Moore, Jennie P. Moore, Rachel R. Pamphlett, Anna Belle Phillips, Marguerite Thompson, and Willie T. Young. In 1938, a new fireproof, 16-room, two-story building was constructed to replace the old wood-frame building. Upon Principal Johnson's retirement, Richard H. Neville was appointed the new principal and served in that capacity until his retirement in 1946. In 1946, Lucile Hansborough Brewer was appointed principal of Klondike. She remained the principal until her promotion to Supervisor of Negro Elementary Schools in Memphis in 1952. Miss Jim Ella Cotton was appointed principal in 1952, and she stayed at Klondike until her promotion to Supervisor of Negro Elementary Schools in Memphis in 1958. Mrs. Anna F. Jones, a teacher at Klondike, was appointed principal in 1958 and served the school in that capacity until her retirement in 1979. Klondike Elementary School is still an active school, currently operating as a public charter school. (Courtesy of The University of Memphis Special Collection)

Elijah H. Triplett was the principal of Klondike School in 1915. Before serving at Klondike, he served as the president of Alcorn A & M College from 1896 to 1899, and he continued to serve as the Professor of History at the college after his presidency. After leaving Alcorn A & M, he served as the county superintendent of negro schools in Lauderdale County, MS. (Courtesy of Alcorn State University Collection)

Lucille Hansborough Brewer, pictured left, served as teacher, principal, and supervisor for the Memphis City School District. A 1918 graduate of Kortrecht High, Mrs. Hansborough Brewer earned a Bachelor of Arts Degree from LeMoyne College. She began her teaching career in 1920. She served as a 5th-grade teacher before being appointed the principal of Klondike Elementary in 1946. She remained at Klondike until 1951 when she was named the Supervisor of Negro Elementary Schools in Memphis. Mrs. Hansborough Brewer was a member of Zeta Phi Beta Sorority, Inc. (Courtesy of a private collection)

Jim Ella Cotton served as the principal of Klondike School from 1952 to 1958. Miss Cotton began her teaching career in Memphis in 1916. She earned a Bachelor of Arts from LeMoyne College in 1933 and a Master of Arts from Columbia University. In addition to her time at Klondike, she served as a teacher at LaRose and Greenwood Schools and Booker T. Washington High School. Her father, J.D. Cotton, taught in Memphis for over 40 years, serving as principal of Greenwood and LaRose Schools. In 1958, she was appointed the Supervisor of Negro Elementary Schools in Memphis. Miss Cotton was a member of Sigma Gamma Rho Sorority, Inc. (Courtesy of a private collection)

Anna F. Jones was a teacher and principal at Klondike Elementary School for over 40 years. Miss Jones earned a Bachelor of Arts Degree from LeMoyne College in 1937 and a master's degree from Columbia University years later. In 1958, she was appointed principal of Klondike when Miss Jim Ella Cotton was promoted to Supervisor of Negro Elementary Schools in Memphis. Principal Jones would remain the principal until her retirement in 1979. (Courtesy of a private collection)

# SPRING HILL GRAMMAR SCHOOL (ROSENWALD)

The Spring Hill School was established in Raleigh, Tennessee around 1905. The Spring Hill Baptist Church purchased the land on which one of the earliest school buildings stood to establish a school. According to an article in the Commercial Appeal Newspaper, Sallie Green and Mattie Smith were the school's teachers in 1908. A school building, constructed with the support of the Rosenwald Fund, was completed between 1918 and 1921. In 1919, Aaben Felton, Carrie Johnson, Felicia Harris, and Mattie Boyd made up the school's faculty, according to the Commercial Appeal. From 1933 to 1938, Cornell Wells served as the principal-teacher at Spring Hill School. From 1939 to 1962, Ira Emery served as the principal teacher, and his wife, Lois Emery, was one of the teachers. By the late 1940s, Spring Hill had grown into a six-room school building and needed more space. In 1952, the school's faculty consisted of Felicia M. Sartin, Willie C. Hollman, Vivian W. Stewart, and Blanche F. Stevenson, who taught at Spring Hill with Principal Ira Emery and Lois Emery. Pictured above is the Spring Hill School in the 1920s. The Spring Hill School building is currently home to a public charter school. (Courtesy of the Fletcher Dresslar Report on the Rosenwald School Buildings No. 1)

In 1956, a newly constructed Spring Hill School building opened. It was a 22-room structure with a cafeteria and had a capacity of 715. Due to court rulings surrounding court-mandated school desegregation, Spring Hill closed at the end of the 1968-1969 school year but reopened in 1970. Pictured below is the building that was constructed in 1956. (Courtesy of the Tennessee State University Special Collection)

Prescott C. Fisher, Sr. was named the principal of Spring Hill in 1962. Fisher was a graduate of Woodstock Training School. Fisher graduated from Tennessee A & I State College in 1940 with a bachelor's degree and earned a master's degree in 1959 from the same college. From 1942 to 1945, he served in the United States Army during WWII, attaining the rank of Sergeant First Class. He taught at White Station Elementary, E.A. Harrold and Collierville Junior High Schools, and Geeter High. He was appointed the principal of Weaver Elementary in 1959, Spring Hill Elementary in 1962, and Mt. Pisgah Elementary years later before retiring in 1978. served as the principal of Eads from 1955 to 1959. (Courtesy of the Tennessee State University Special Collection)

# CARNES ELEMENTARY SCHOOL

The first Carnes School opened in 1899, with Charles J. Neal as its first head teacher. Carnes School was established to serve the African American youth bordered by Manassas Street, Poplar Avenue, and Old Raleigh Road. As a grammar school, Carnes served grades one through eight. According to the Commercial Appeal, 229 students were enrolled in September 1899. In 1904, Charles Neal was promoted from headteacher to principal at Carnes. Pictured above is Carnes School, which was constructed in 1904. (Courtesy of the Memphis Public Library & Information Center) The photograph was taken in the early 1920s. Below is a student group from Carnes that placed second in the City Beautiful Contest in the late 1940s. (Courtesy of a private collection)

In 1907, the following teachers made up the faculty at Carnes School: R. H. Neville, Bertha E. Jones, Lucie E. Campbell, Marie L. McCulloch, Susie C. Yancy, Minnie E. Allen, Electa E. Wright, Mattie H. Bell, Cora E. Sutton, Alice M. Taylor, Blanche Neal, and Beatrice Edwards. Professor Charles Neal served as the principal of Carnes Elementary until he died in 1934. During his time at Carnes, a new teacher named Miss Lucie E. Campbell began her teaching career under his leadership. In 1939, a new building was completed to replace the old wood frame building that opened in 1904. In the 1910s and 1920s, the city's dump and morgue were behind the Carnes School. In 1926, the following teachers made up the faculty of Carnes School: C.J. Neal, principal; Mattie Bell, Helen Broome, Elizabeth Cotton, Lillian Dupree, Lucy Fowlkes, Viola Hudson, Helen White Jenkins, Evelyn V. Johnson, M.L. Jones, Addie Love, Esther P. Luster, Graftie Mosby, Audrey Nelson, Anna Nicholson, Ethel R. Threlkeld, Geneva Threlkeld, Annie Thomas, and Alice M. Winchester. Pictured above are students on the school's grounds in the late 1940's. (Courtesy of a private collection)

In 1934, Alonzo Love was named principal. The Commercial Appeal named the following Carnes's faculty in 1936: Mattie Bell, Lillian Carnes, Elizabeth M. Cotton, Annie L. Flake, Lucy G. Fowlkes, Annie Franklin, Willie Mae Hawkins, Alam Hobson, Myrtle Hudson, Lottye V. Irwin, Evely Johnson, Addie Love, Esther Luster, Anna Nicholson, Juanita Perkins, Cornelia Sanders, Ethel Threlkeld, Willie L. Tillman, and Mabel Washburn. Professor E.C. Jones, principal of LaRose Elementary, was appointed principal of Carnes following the death of Professor Love in 1940. Three additional buildings were added to the school's campus in the 1950s. Carnes Elementary School closed in 2018. Pictured above is Carnes Grammar School in the 1940s. Pictured below are Carnes Students playing a game of baseball with the Tom Lee Swimming Pool in the background. (Courtesy of a private collection)

Charles Julius Neal, Sr. was one of the first head teachers/principals of Carnes School. He was an 1881 high school graduate of the LeMoyne Institute and earned a degree from the school. According to school board records, he served as a teacher at the Lucy Avenue School until 1899, when he was elected head teacher at Carnes School. During the 1890s, Professor Neal served as the president of The Colored Teachers' Institute of Shelby County. From 1925 to 1926, he served as the president of the Tennessee Education Congress. This appointment made him the second president ever of the statewide organization. He retired in 1934 after serving 35 years at Carnes. Sadly, he died just a few weeks after retiring. (Courtesy of the Tennessee State University Special Collection)

Pictured left is Edwin Chappelle "E.C." Jones. Professor Jones was appointed principal of Carnes in 1940. Born and raised in Memphis, Jones attended Wilberforce University before beginning his career as a teacher in North Carolina. In the late 1920s, he was hired as a science teacher at Booker T. Washington High School under the leadership of G.P. Hamilton. Within a few years, he was promoted to assistant principal. Professor Jones was a member of Alpha Phi Alpha Fraternity, Inc. (Courtesy of a private collection)

# HYDE PARK ELEMENTARY SCHOOL

The Hyde Park School opened in the early 1920s in the Hyde Park neighborhood in Memphis. Until the 1920s, the Hyde Park Community was outside the city limits. James L. Buckner was the school's principal during the late 1920s and mid-1930s. Professor William Alexander Lynk, Sr. was Hyde Park's principal in 1936 when they opened a new school building on Tunica Street. That building had 22 classrooms and an auditorium. That year, the following teachers made up the faculty of Hyde Park School: William A. Lynk, principal; Louise Barrentine, Callie Branch, Sarah O. Brown, Osville L. Cash, Geneva Corthoran, Naomi Creswell, Irene Dawson, Susie Hightower, Mildred Johnson, Nannie Little, May Ella Lundy, Callie McGuire, Ethel McQueen, Alice Morris, Mamie Pamphlett, Edwina Porter, and Carrie Stiggall.

In 1946, Andrew Benjamin Bland was appointed principal. He has the distinction of serving as principal on two separate occasions. Bland first served as principal from 1946 to 1956. After transferring to Lester High School as principal in 1956, he would return to Hyde Park in 1959 as principal and would remain at the school until his retirement in 1970. When Principal Bland was at Lester High, Melvin Conley served as principal from 1956 to 1957. The appointment of principal was Mr. Conley's first, and he would go on to serve as the principal of Porter Junior High and Melrose High School. From 1957 to 1959, Samuel Helm, a former teacher at Douglass High, served as the school's principal. When Principal Bland retired in 1970, Joseph Wilkerson was named Hyde Park's principal.

The city's forced busing strategy to desegregate Memphis City Schools, forced several schools, including Hyde Park Elementary, to close in 1973. Pictured above is Hyde Park Elementary School in the 1940s. (Courtesy of The University of Memphis Special Collection)

Principal James Lowell Buckner served as the principal of Hyde Park School during the mid-1920s and early 1930's. Before leading Hyde Park, he was a teacher at Manassas High and Kortrecht High and served as the principal of Magnolia School. In addition to his time at Hyde Park School, Professor Buckner was the principal of Kortrecht Grammar, Carnes, and Hamilton High Schools. He retired in 1953 after 40 years of service to public schools in Memphis. (Courtesy of the Tennessee State University Special Collection)

Samuel Helm served as Hyde Park principal from 1957 to 1959. Principal Helm was a 1947 graduate of LeMoyne College. Before graduating from LeMoyne, he served in the United States Army as a Master Sergeant during WWII from 1942 to 1945. He began his career in education as a teacher at Douglass High School. In 1959, he was appointed the principal of the new Shannon Elementary in North Memphis. He would remain at Shannon until his retirement in 1977. (Courtesy of a private collection)

# ST. STEPHEN SCHOOL

St. Stephen Elementary School was established in the Berclair community in 1930 under the direction of St. Stephen Baptist Church leaders. The school served students in grades 1-8. According to records, the school building, pictured above, was built in 1930 on property that included the church. The building was a wood-frame building with outdoor toilets and water. In 1950, the Commercial Appeal reported that St. Stephen Baptist Church and Berclair Civic Club members wanted to build homes on land behind the church. The school closed in 1952 after enrollment had fallen to just 29 students due to white development in the area. The photograph above is of the former St. Stephen School Building. Today, the building is home to a daycare center.

Dovie Rogers Burnley, pictured left in the 1940's1940s, was the principal of St. Stephen School during the 1940's1940s and early 1950's1950s. She served at St. Stephen until the school's closing in 1952. She was a 1947 graduate of LeMoyne College, earning a Bachelor of Arts Degree. After her time at St. Stephen, she was named principal at Dunn Elementary. Mrs. Burnley served as Dunn Elementary School's principal until she retired in 1977. Mrs. Burnley was a member of Zeta Phi Beta Sorority, Inc. (Courtesy of a private collection)

Joe Gentry, Jr., pictured left, was a student at St. Stephen School. As a seventh-grade student, he was the St. Stephen's Spelling Bee Champion and the runner-up in the Memphis Press Scimitar's 24th Annual Shelby County Black Spelling Bee in 1952. Gentry was also the school's spelling bee champion in 1951. After the school's closing, he attended Lester, where he excelled as a student and became the school's spelling bee champ. Mr. Gentry was a 1957 graduate of Manassas High School, a 1961 graduate of Mississippi Industrial College in Holly Springs, MS, and completed his graduate studies at Purdue University. He began his career in education in 1961 as a teacher at Shannon Elementary. When the Memphis City School District started desegregating its schools, Mr. Gentry was among the teachers who helped make this transition work. Before his retirement after 33 years of service, Mr. Gentry taught at Coro Lake, Graves, and Springdale Elementary Schools. (Courtesy of the Gentry Family)

# SHANNON ELEMENTARY SCHOOL

Shannon Elementary opened in 1959 in the Hollywood Community in North Memphis. The building, pictured above, was a one-story brick building with 34 rooms, including cafetorium and offices. The school's first principal was Samuel W. Helm. Former Mayor of Memphis and Memphis City School District Superintendent Dr. Willie. W. Herenton served as a teacher at Shannon Elementary. In 1977, Mr. Halloe Robinson was named principal of the school. He replaced Mr. Helm, who retired. Mr. Robinson remained at Shannon until 1987. During his time, he inspired many students at Shannon Elementary, including the author of this book. According to the Commercial Appeal, in 1970, an active dump was just 100 yards away from the school. The city of Memphis began using the dump in 1962 and ceased its use years later, but illegal dumps continued. In 1980, there were concerns about the pesticide chlordane being found in the soil of the school's playground. Shannon Elementary closed as a school within the Shelby County School District in 2014. (Courtesy of Google Maps)

Samuel Helm was appointed the first principal of Shannon Elementary in 1959. Previously, he served as the Hyde Park principal from 1957 to 1959. Principal Helm was a 1947 graduate of LeMoyne College. Before graduating from LeMoyne, he served in the United States Army as a Master Sergeant during WWII from 1942 to 1945. He began his career in education as a teacher at Douglass High School. (Courtesy of a private collection)

Halloe Odell Robinson, pictured left as a student at Tennessee A & I State College, served as the principal of Shannon Elementary from 1977 to 1987. Mr. Robinson was a long-time resident of the Douglass Community and a 1955 graduate of Douglass High School. In 1959, he graduated with a Bachelor of Science in Education from Tennessee A & I State College, and he earned a Master of Education degree in Guidance and Counseling from Memphis State University in 1969. During his tenure with the Memphis City School District, Mr. Robinson was a teacher, guidance counselor, and assistant principal. When he was appointed to Shannon Elementary, Mr. Robinson was serving as the assistant principal at Frayser High School. Mr. Robinson became Specialist 4th Class in the United States Army during the Vietnam War. Halloe O. Robinson was a member of Phi Beta Sigma Fraternity, Inc. (Courtesy of the Tennessee State University Special Collection)

# Chapter Four

# Schools in Northeast Shelby County (Bartlett, Brunswick, Eads, Arlington, Barretville, and Cordova)

## BARRET'S CHAPEL HIGH SCHOOL (ROSENWALD)

Barret's Chapel High School was the first high school established for African American children in Northern Shelby County. Originally named Hayes Grove, the school was first mentioned in the Commercial Appeal newspaper in 1907, with Vivian Bolton as the principal. Her monthly salary was $35. According to Shelby County Board records, Edward Gray was the principal of Hayes Grove in 1924, and Ezzia Woods, Allie Ruth Davis, and Constance Bolton served as the school's other teachers. An eight-room building was built on the site of the current school in 1925, and Grades 9 through 12 were added. The school was renamed Barret's Chapel High School that year after James Howell "J.H." Barret, who helped establish the school. The school's first senior class held its graduation in 1929, with five students receiving their diplomas. The following educators also served as school principals between 1925 and 1968: James T. Trail, Ira R. Emery, and Guy Hoffman. (Courtesy of the Tennessee State University Special Collection)

The desegregation of schools impacted Barret's Chapel, and its last senior class graduated in 1971. With the high school closed, the school served students from kindergarten through grade eight. In 1952, the following teachers were members of the Barret's Chapel Faculty: Guy E. Hoffman, Principal, M.V. Allen, Alma Anderson, Constance Bolton, Mary A. Cherry, J.N. Cunningham, Ophelia Gilbert, Ralph Haynes, Rheba Hoffman, Harry M. Johnson, Hattie Johnson, Yolander Kirksey, Alpina Lewis, Tinnie Smith, L.C. Suttles, Lucy Suttles, Juanita Wherry, Jimmie Woodard, Mary A. Wright, Faye Yuill, and George Yuill. Pictured below is the Barret's Chapel Marching Band. Pictured above is Barret's Chapel High in the 1960s. (Courtesy of Julia Earle Williamson). The photo below is of the Barret's Chapel Marching Band in the 1960s. (Courtesy of Florenstine S. Woods)

Professor Guy Elliott Hoffman became the principal of Barret's Chapel in 1928. He served as principal until his retirement in 1968. Like most principals of the day, Mr. Hoffman served as a teacher and coach in addition to his principal duties. Before serving at Barret's Chapel, he taught at the Shelby County Training School and Manassas High School. A 1926 Tennessee A & I State College graduate, Hoffman was a star football athlete and captain of the football team. He also earned a Master of Science in Educational Administration from Tennessee A & I College in 1958. From 1918 to 1919, Mr. Hoffman served overseas in the United States Army during WWI, reaching the rank of private. He and his wife, Rheba Hoffman, retired in 1968 after serving the students in Shelby County for 40 years. (Courtesy of the Tennessee State University Special Collection)

Mrs. Rheba Palmer Hoffman began teaching at Barret's Chapel in 1926 alongside her husband, Principal Guy E. Hoffman. Pictured left, as a student at Tennessee A & I State College, Hoffman was a 1926 graduate of the college. A writer and civic leader, she also graduated from Atlanta University with a master's degree in library science. Following her retirement in 1968, she served as a Shelby County School Board member. (Courtesy of the Tennessee State University Special Collection)

Ralph S. Haynes, pictured left, served as a mathematics teacher, assistant principal, and principal of Barret's Chapel High. He was hired by Principal Hoffman in 1952. Before arriving at Barret's Chapel, Mr. Haynes served in the United States Navy beginning in 1944. He earned a Bachelor of Science in Mathematics from Tennessee A & I State College in 1952 and a Master of Science in Mathematics from Atlanta University in 1960. In addition to his duties at Barret's Chapel, he served as the Shelby County Director of the Head Start Program and the supervisor of the Adult Education Program. Following the retirement of Principal Hoffman, he was appointed the principal and served in that capacity from 1968 to 1983. (Courtesy of Florenstine S. Woods)

Reverend Finis Fields, Sr. served as a teacher at Barret's Chapel during the 1950's and 1960's. Before teaching at Barret's Chapel, Rev. Fields taught in Fayette County. A 1950 graduate of Lane College in Jackson, TN, Fields served in the United States Army during WWII, where he reached the rank of TEC 4 or Sergeant. He was appointed assistant principal of Collierville Elementary in 1967 and served in other capacities with the Shelby County School District, including pupil services supervisor, before his retirement in 1980. A civic leader, Rev. Fields served as a Shelby County School Board member from 1984 to 1997 and the pastor of Oak Spring Baptist Church in Arlington from 1972 to 1999. He was a lifetime member of the NAACP and a member of Alpha Phi Alpha Fraternity, Inc. (Courtesy of the Lane College Collection)

# EADS JUNIOR HIGH SCHOOL
## (ROSENWALD)

One of the first schools in Eads for African Americans was established around 1908 when Suvella Robinson Benton was the teacher. In 1918, Eads Jr. High School was built with support from the Rosenwald Fund. The school was located on US Highway 64 near Collierville-Arlington Road. Eads Jr. High School served students in grades 1 through 10. E.A. Teague served as the school's principal in 1918, making him the first principal of the new school. Over the years, several improvements were made to the school. In 1953, the Shelby County School Board approved the construction of two new classrooms, indoor restrooms, and a cafeteria. These additions were made while Searcy Cornelius Harris was the school's principal. (Courtesy of the Tennessee State University Special Collection)

Principal Searcy Harris was a 1933 Tennessee A & I State College graduate. He also earned a Master of Education degree from New York University. Before being appointed to Eads, Harris taught agriculture at Neshoba Junior High and was the principal of Ellendale Elementary. He served as the agricultural teacher and principal at Eads for several years. During his tenure at Eads, approximately 350 students were enrolled annually. He was named the principal of the newly constructed Mt. Pisgah High School in 1955. He remained at Mt. Pisgah High until his retirement in 1970. Pictured above is the school in the early 1950's. Isaiah J. Graham, Jr. served as the principal of Eads from 1959 to his death in 1960. In 1960, John Strong, Jr. was appointed the principal of Eads Junior High. He served at the school from 1960-1962. Sam Lucas served as the principal until 1966, and Vernie L. Jones was appointed principal in 1966. Principal Jones graduated from Tennessee State University, earning a Bachelor of Science degree in Agriculture education in 1954 and a Master of Arts in Education degree in 1972. He served as the principal until 1968.

Eads Junior High School consolidated with Mt. Pisgah High School in 1970. After its closure, the building was used to house the Eads Head Start Center and a Shelby County Health Clinic from 1973-2001. The building was demolished in 2016. The picture above is the school building near the time of its demolition. (Courtesy of a private collection)

Elihu A. "E.A." Teague was the first principal of Eads Junior High School. He began his career in education by serving as the teaching principal at the Baptist Industrial College in DeSoto County, MS, where his father, Rev. Alexander L. Teague, was one of the school's founders. Teague served at the school for two years before becoming the principal of Eads Junior High School. He led Eads School from around 1915 to 1925 when he was elected a teacher at Manassas High School. He retired in 1959 after 34 years of service to the students and faculty of Manassas High School. (Courtesy of a private collection)

Prescott C. Fisher, Sr. served as the principal of Eads from 1955 to 1959. He previously served as an agricultural teacher at Geeter High School. Principal Fisher was a graduate of Woodstock Training School. He graduated from Tennessee A & I State College in 1940 with a bachelor's degree and earned a master's degree in 1959 from the same college. From 1942 to 1945, Fisher served in the United States Army during WWII, attaining the rank of Sergeant First Class. He taught at White Station Elementary, E.A. Harrold and Collierville Junior High Schools, and Geeter High. He was appointed the principal of Weaver Elementary in 1959, Spring Hill Elementary in 1962, and Mt. Pisgah Elementary years later before retiring in 1978. (Courtesy of the Tennessee State University Special Collection)

# ANTHONY CHAPEL SCHOOL

Anthony Chapel School was established in 1928 to serve the students of the Barretville, Mudville, and Rosemark Communities in Northern Shelby County. The school was named after the grandfather of the Shelby County School Board Member Paul Barret, Sr. Located on Mulberry Road and adjacent to the Strong Family Farm, the wood-frame school consisted of two rooms. According to former student John E. Strong, Jr., the brownish-red building was heated with a potbellied, coal-burning stove. In one room, children in grades one through three would learn together, while students in grades four through eight would learn in the other room. For recreation, there was a large playground behind the school. Like most schools at the time, the school day started with devotion before reading, grammar, and math instruction began. After completing grade 8, students would have to walk several miles or board with family or neighbors to attend Barret's Chapel High School to complete grades 9-12.

Pictured left is the first principal of Anthony Chapel School, Mertus S. Strong, Sr. He is pictured with his wife, Ida. According to records, Principal Strong also taught at Hayes Grove School (later renamed Barret's Chapel School). He received his early school instruction at a Presbyterian Church near his childhood home. Professor Strong served as the school's principal until his retirement in 1937. (Courtesy of John E. Strong, Jr.)

Lois Mae Strong Emery served as a teacher and principal of Anthony Chapel School. With her husband, Ira, she taught at the school alongside her father, Professor Mertus S. Strong, Sr. Following their time at Anthony Chapel School, she and Ira were appointed to Spring Hill Elementary School. Mrs. Strong was a graduate of the Mississippi Industrial College in Holly Springs, MS. (Courtesy of John E. Strong, Jr.)

Ira R. Emery served as a teacher and principal at Anthony Chapel School. Born in Yazoo City, MS, Professor Emery also served as the principal of Bush Grove and Log Union Schools. Both schools were near present-day Lakeland, TN. He and his wife taught together at Anthony Chapel School and Spring Hill School for more than 30 years. He retired as principal of Spring Hill School in 1961. (Courtesy of John E. Strong, Jr.)

Professor John Strong, Jr., who served as the principal of Eads, Weaver, Capleville High, and Woodstock High, attended Anthony's Chapel as a child. He is also the grandson of Mertus S. Strong, Sr., and nephew of Ira Emery and Lois Strong Emery. He attended the school from grades 1 through 8 before graduating from Barret's Chapel High School. (Courtesy of Rev. Dr. Clennon Saulsberry, Sr.)

# BRIDGEWATER SCHOOL
# (ROSENWALD)

The Bridgewater School was established in the early 1900s. In 1908, the Commercial Appeal Newspaper listed Alice Bernard as the principal of Bridgewater School. With the support of the Rosenwald Fund, an addition was built onto the school in 1918. Located on Raleigh-LaGrange Road, the school was bordered by Appling, Macon, and Dexter Roads. Records indicate that the first wood-frame structure was painted red and had two rooms. According to the Commercial Appeal, the following teachers served at Bridgewater School in 1919: Josephine Simpson, Susie Smith, and Jennie McCulley. In 1924, Georgia Sylvers served as the principal, and Pearl Chatman, Rosa Ford, Lucy Clemons Newborn, and Alma Roach served as teachers. Mrs. Sylvers served as a math teacher at Manassas High School and principal at Bridgewater for more than 40 years before she retired in 1960. She remained at Bridgewater for 12 years before retiring.

In 1952, Lucille Crawford was the principal, and Katie Coopwood and Carrie Crawford served as teachers. According to a 1952 article in the Memphis Press-Scimitar Newspaper, the school was one of the poorest schools in the county, and its interior had never been painted during its first 34 years of existence. Georgia Rose Sylvers served as the principal of Bridgewater during the 1920's and 1930's. Mrs. Sylvers was a graduate of the LeMoyne Institute. At the time of her retirement, she was a math teacher at Manassas High School. (Courtesy of a private collection)

Bridgewater School merged with Mt. Pisgah in 1960. Today, the schoolhouse, standing a less than a block of block of Dexter Middle School, is a private residence.

# BRUNSWICK JUNIOR HIGH SCHOOL (ROSENWALD)

Brunswick Junior High School was established in Brunswick, TN around 1923. It is one of the many schools in Shelby County that was built in partnership with the Rosenwald Fund. In the school's early years, Brunswick was a four-teacher school, but when a shop room was added a few years later, the faculty increased to five teachers. In 1924, William I. Trotter served as the principal with Sallie Belote, Susie Martin, Shellie Martin, Ora Hammond, and Theresa Horton making up the remainder of the faculty. The year 1952 brought new improvements to the school. According to Commercial Appeal, the following improvements were made in 1952: a new agriculture and home economics rooms, two new classrooms, an enlarged auditorium, a new well pump, gas heat, and an electric water heater and stove. Pictured above is the school in the early 1950s. (Courtesy of the Tennessee State University Special Collection). Below is the school building today, which a neighboring church now owns. (Courtesy of a private collection)

The faculty of the school during the 1952 year consisted of Principal Edward Gray, Mrs. Annie B. Coleman, Miss Jean Farrow, Mrs. Bessie Gray, Mr. J. S. Mebane, Mrs. Gertrude Settles, Mr. James Scott, Mr. John Strong, Jr., Miss Inez Taylor, Mrs. H.G. Wimble, and Mrs. Clorine Webb. James Nelson Scott began his career in education as a teacher at Brunswick Junior High School in 1952. Mr. Scott was a graduate of Allen White High School in Hardeman County, TN. After graduating, he served in the United States Navy during WWII from 1943 to 1946. Scott graduated from Lane College in 1952. He went on to teach and coach at Mt. Pisgah High School and Collierville High School before retiring. He was a member of Alpha Phi Alpha Fraternity, Inc.

Brunswick Junior High School consolidated with nearby Shadowlawn School in 1966. The girls' basketball team with coach Mrs. Bessie Gray in 1952 is pictured above. (Courtesy of the Tennessee State University Special Collection)

Edward E. Gray served as the principal of Brunswick Junior High School. He graduated from Lane College and completed graduate work at Tennessee A & I State University. Mr. Gray and his wife, Bessie Gray, taught at Brunswick and continued at Shadowlawn when they were appointed to positions there. He was a member of the Brunswick and Ellendale Civic Clubs and the fraternal order of Accepted and Free Masons. (Courtesy of the Tennessee State University Special Collection)

Junious S. Mebane, pictured left, was appointed the Brunswick Jr. High principal in 1961. Mr. Mebane was a 1927 graduate of Tennessee A & I State College. For many years, he was an agricultural teacher at several schools in rural Shelby County, including Brunswick Junior and Bartlett Junior High Schools. A member of Alpha Phi Alpha Fraternity, Inc., Mebane retired after 39 years of service to Shelby County Schools. (Courtesy of the Tennessee State University Special Collection)

# ARLINGTON SCHOOL (ROSENWALD)

The Arlington School was first mentioned in the Commercial Appeal Newspaper in 1908 with Effie Hays, a teacher, and Estelle Hegler, an assistant. In 1909, Alfred Clarke was recorded as a principal-teacher at Arlington with Estelle Hegler as the assistant. In 1918, a new school was built with the support of the Rosenwald Fund. The building was a three-room school with a multipurpose room. With Cecil Sales as the principal, Ida Branch, Lucile Slack, Rowena Dandridge, and Virgie Hayes made up the remainder of the school's faculty in the 1924 school year. Annie Logan, a teacher at Gailor High School in Tipton County for many years, also served as a teacher at the Arlington School in the late 1920s. In 1934, John Lyphas Hill was appointed principal. He remained at Arlington for the next 23 years until 1957, when Joseph Simmons, a teacher at Geeter High School, was appointed principal. Mr. John Hill was appointed principal in 1961 when Principal Simmons accepted the principal position at Neshoba Junior High. As a result of school desegregation, the school closed in 1970, and the school district transferred the students to Arlington Elementary School, then located on Chester Street. Pictured above is the Arlington School building, part of a commercial business complex on Arline Road in Arlington, TN. (Courtesy of a private collection)

Pictured left is Joseph Simmons, former principal of Arlington Elementary School from 1957 to 1961. He began his career in education as a 5th-grade teacher at Geeter School in Memphis. Before his time teaching, he served in the United States Army during WWII from 1942 to 1946. He returned to Memphis and enrolled at Geeter High School as a senior. He attended Tennessee A & I State University in Nashville, TN, where he graduated in 1950 with a Bachelor of Science in Agriculture and again in 1965 when he earned a Master of Education Degree in Administration and Supervision. While at Tennessee State University, he became a member of Phi Beta Sigma Fraternity, Inc. He left Arlington in 1961 when he was appointed the principal at Neshoba Jr. High in Germantown. Additionally, he led Capleville High School and White's Chapel Elementary before retiring. (Courtesy of Rev. Dr. Clennon Saulsberry, Sr.)

# MT. PISGAH SCHOOL
# (ROSENWALD)

Mt. Pisgah School was established around 1908. Shelby County School Board minutes from 1908, James W. Hewlett was the school's principal. In 1919, the Commercial Appeal indicated that the following teachers made up the faculty of Mt. Pisgah School: Fannie Beason, A. L. Davis, and Nora Grey. During the 1924 school year, the following teachers were assigned to Mt. Pisgah: William C. Tyus (Principal), Laura Tyus, Eliza Anderson, Catherine Twine, and Ary Bailey. In 1952, two teachers, including the principal, comprised the school's faculty: Mrs. Addie Stafford, principal, and Mrs. Frances D. Hooks. The school served students in grades 1 through 6. According to the Memphis Press-Scimitar Newspaper, Mt. Pisgah did not have toilets, water, or lights in 1952. The eighty-two students enrolled at the school used outdoor toilets at a nearby church, and they got their water from a neighbor's well. In 1955, the county constructed a new building to replace the old wood-frame Mt. Pisgah School building. The new school building had 16 classrooms and a cafeteria. The school served students in grades 1 through 12. In 1955, Mr. Searcy C. Harris was appointed the principal of the new Mt. Pisgah High School. He previously served as the principal of Eads Junior High. Searcy Harris retired in 1970. Mt. Pisgah School remains active in Shelby County, serving students in grades 6 through 8.

William C. Tyus, Sr. served as the principal of Mt. Pisgah School during the 1920s. He graduated from Rust College in Holly Springs, MS., and began his teaching career in Shelby County at Eads Junior High School in 1919. Before that time, Tyus taught in Trenton, TN, and Crawfordsville, AR. After leaving Mt. Pisgah, he taught mathematics at Booker T. Washington High School for 32 years before retiring in 1960. His late wife, Laura Tyus, taught with him at Mt. Pisgah School. (Courtesy of a private collection)

# SHADOWLAWN JUNIOR HIGH SCHOOL

Shadowlawn High School opened in the fall of 1958. The school, located on Shadowlawn Road in Bartlett, was a modern 12-room building that initially served students in grades 1 through 8. Edward Equilla Gray served as the school's first principal. Principal Gray previously served as the principal of Brunswick Junior High School. In July of 1964, a lightning strike started a fire that destroyed several classrooms and damaged several other spaces, including the cafeteria. Students completed the 1964-1965 school year in a temporary building while the damaged building was rebuilt. In 1965, a new building was completed. The new building provided twenty-four new classrooms to be added to the six rooms saved from the fire. During the spring of 1966, the cafeteria staff at Shadowlawn prepared hot lunches for the Bartlett Junior High School students, which did not have a cafeteria. During the 1966-67 school year, a plan was approved to make Shadowlawn a high school. In 1967, a new addition was completed to accommodate ninth-grade students. The following year, another classroom addition and gymnasium were completed to support the addition of tenth-grade students. In 1969-70, eleventh grade was added to the school. Unfortunately, Shadowlawn High School never had a graduating class as the school was ordered to close when Shelby County Schools were desegregated in 1970. The students at Shadowlawn High School were bused to the formerly all-white Bartlett High School. Ultimately, Shadowlawn returned to being a junior high school that now served both black and white students. In 2014, Shadowlawn Middle School was converted into the Bartlett Freshman Academy. It remains an active school today. The photo above is of Shadowlawn School in the early 1970s. (Courtesy of a private collection)

Edward E. Gray served as the principal of Brunswick Junior High School. He graduated from Lane College and took graduate work at Tennessee A & I State University. Gray and his wife, Bessie, taught at Brunswick and continued at Shadowlawn when he was appointed principal in April 1958. He served as Shadowlawn's principal until 1967.

Dr. Samuel Lucas served as the principal of Shadowlawn Junior High from 1967 to 1968. He earned a bachelor's degree from Alcorn State University in 1952 and a master's degree in education from the University of Tennessee at Knoxville in 1967. He served as an agricultural teacher at Woodstock High School for several years. He was appointed the principal of Eads Junior High in 1962, replacing John Strong, Jr. who had been appointed the principal of Weaver Elementary. After leaving Shadowlawn, Principal Lucas earned a doctoral degree in education from the University of Tennessee and served as a director and professor at several universities, including the University of Tennessee, Memphis State University, and Tennessee State University. (Courtesy of the University of Memphis Special Collection)

# WELLS SCHOOL
# (ROSENWALD)

The Wells School was first established around 1908. According to the Commercial Appeal, Cecil Sales was the principal of Wells School in 1908. A second building, located along Airline Road in Eads, TN, was constructed with assistance from the Rosenwald Fund in 1924. Records indicate that the school building was originally a two-room, wood-frame structure and served students in first through eighth grades. An additional room was added to the school years later. In 1924, Mattie McNeese served as the principal, and Callie Ingram was the second teacher. In 1952, Marilou Phillips and Effie Shaw were teachers, with Aaron Jones serving as the principal. Effie Shaw was appointed the principal of Wells when Mr. Aaron P. Jones retired in 1962. The school was consolidated with nearby Mt. Pisgah School in 1966. The school building was placed on the National Register of Historic Places in 1995. To this day, the schoolhouse stands as a residential property. (Courtesy of private collection)

# HOME FERRY GRAMMAR SCHOOL (ROSENWALD)

The Home Ferry School was located at Osborntown Road and Pleasant Ridge Road just south of Millington-Arlington Road. Home Ferry School was a three-room, wood-frame structure. The school was mentioned for the first time in the Commercial Appeal Newspaper in 1907. At that time, Norah Thomas was the school's principal. In 1909, records indicate that Sam Hill was Home Ferry's principal. In 1919, Currie E. Stewart and Helen Albright were listed as Home Ferry's teachers. A new school building was constructed with the support of the Rosenwald Fund in 1923. At that time, Miss Estell Heglar was the school's principal, and Dora Braden was the second teacher. When Home Ferry closed in 1952, Principal John L. Hill was appointed the principal of Arlington Elementary. The photo above is of the Home Ferry Schoolhouse, built in 1923. (Courtesy of Memphis Landmarks Commission)

# FULLVIEW SCHOOL
# (ROSENWALD)

The Fullview School was located near the Fullview Baptist Church in Ellendale, TN, on Memphis-Arlington Road near Oak Road. Situated near the church's cemetery, the original school was a wood-frame single-story structure with one or two rooms. The Fullview School was first mentioned in the Commercial Appeal Newspaper in 1907. That year, George W. Thomas was the school's teacher. Mr. Thomas, a farmer and teacher, also served as the school's teacher in 1908. In 1909, Pastor John Barnett served as the school's principal, and Mrs. Osceola W. Alexander was the assistant teacher. By 1919, three teachers were assigned to the school: Edmonia L. Taylor, Alice Harper, and Audrey Nelson Williams. In 1924, the faculty of Fullview comprised the following teachers: Obediah H. Gray, principal; Marquerite Hunt Ewing, Willie M. Hawkins; and Ethel Gray, daughter of Principal Gray. Mr. Gray was also the father of Brunswick Jr. High and Shadowlawn High principal Edward E. Gray. According to the Memphis and Shelby County Office of Planning and Development Comprehensive Planning, the Fullview School received a one-room addition in 1925, and a new building was constructed in 1930. The Fullview School closed in 1959.

Edmonia L. Taylor was a teacher at Fullview School during the 1919 school year. According to the Commercial Appeal, Mrs. Taylor began teaching in 1913. Born in Cordova, TN, she attended grade and high school at LeMoyne. Ms. Taylor earned a bachelor's degree from Rust College after she began teaching. During her 49 years as a teacher, Taylor taught at Manassas and Melrose High Schools. She died in 1998 at the age of 105. (Courtesy of a private collection)

# BARTLETT JR. HIGH SCHOOL
# (ROSENWALD)

Once located on Shelby Road in Bartlett, TN, Bartlett School served students in grades 1-8 in a five-room, wood-frame building. According to the Commercial Appeal, Rouchelle Pinkston and Estella Knox served as the school's teachers in 1907. Pinkston's monthly salary was $35, and Knox earned $30 monthly. School board records list Professor Johnson as the school's principal in 1909. Malinda Simpson was the school's principal in 1919, and Grace Johnson and Lassie McCulley served as teachers. The Commercial Appeal Newspaper listed Clara Prince as Bartlett's principal that year, with the following teachers making up the school's faculty: Justine Broglin, Helen Albright, Octavia Nelson, Emma Price, and Bessie Nichols. Henry Grinner served as the last principal of Bartlett Jr. High. During the school's final years, he led the community's fight to keep the school open and add a cafeteria to the school. It was decided that a cafeteria should not be built, and students ate hot lunches prepared at Shadowlawn School and delivered to Bartlett during the final months of the 1965-1966 school year. Bartlett Jr. High closed in 1966, and its students were transferred to various schools in Bartlett.

# PROSPERITY GRAMMAR SCHOOL
# (ROSENWALD)

Prosperity School was located in Shelby County on Old Brownsville Road and Austin Peay Highway. Prosperity School was first mentioned in the Commercial Appeal in 1907 when it noted that Mr. Thomas W. Johnson was elected as the school's teacher. In 1909, G. W. Thomas and Solly Bentley were teachers at Prosperity. According to a 1952 article in the Memphis Press-Scimitar, Prosperity was a two-teacher school that stood on piers. At that time, about 75 students were enrolled at the school. Like most Rosenwald Schools, the schoolhouse was heated with coal in potbellied stoves. According to 1924 school board records, the following teachers made up the staff of Prosperity School: Narcissa Hart, principal, Armenia Franklin, and Jennie Breathett. Prosperity School closed in 1959.

# GILFIELD GRAMMAR SCHOOL
# (ROSENWALD)

According to the Commercial Appeal, the Gilfield School was established around 1908 when Susie Mosely was the elected teacher. The school was located on Pleasant Ridge Road near Donnell Road in Northeast Shelby County. The school building was a two-room, wood-frame structure. S. A. Robinson and Orelia Strong were the school's teachers in 1919. Gilfield and Mt. Sinai, Home Ferry, Benjestown, Bolton, Bottom, Hickory Hill, Walsh, and Forest Hill received a new school building with support from the Rosenwald Fund in 1923. In 1924, Mattie L. Smith was the school's principal, and Bessie Robinson was the school's second teacher. Mrs. Climmie Holmes Pilot, principal, and Mrs. Susie M. Hammond were the two teachers assigned to Gilfield in 1952. Gilfield Grammar School closed in 1959.

# OAK GROVE GRAMMAR SCHOOL
# (ROSENWALD)

The Oak Grove School was located near Bartlett, TN, on TN Highway 64, near TN Highway 70. The school was a three-room, wood-frame structure. The Commercial Appeal Newspaper first mentioned the Oak Grove School in 1907. That year, Mary Homer was a teacher at the school. In 1909, Roschella Pinkston served as the school's teacher. By 1919, two teachers were assigned to the school: Ada Mullins and Fannie Porter. In 1924, the faculty of Oak Grove comprised the following teachers: Ada Mullins, principal, Maggie B. Frazier, Minnie L. Becton, and Mary Greenlaw. The year 1924 also marked the first year that Miss Minnie L. Becton served at Oak Grove. She taught at Oak Grove and Shadowlawn from 1924 to 1968. Miss Katie Rogers was the school's principal in 1944. Oak Grove Grammar School closed in 1958.

# SHADY GROVE GRAMMAR SCHOOL
## (ROSENWALD)

The Shady Grove Grammar School was located on Donnell Road and Austin Peay Highway (Hwy 14) just north of Millington-Arlington Road. Shady Grove School was first mentioned in the Commercial Appeal in 1907 when Mrs. Hattie Stewart Bolton was named the principal. She was the teaching principal at Shady Grove in 1907 and 1909. In 1908, the Shelby County School Board barred married women from serving as teachers. In 1919, Miss Euphema Hall served as the school's principal. During the 1924 school year, the Commercial Appeal listed Currie E. Stewart, brother of Hattie Stewart Bolton, as the school's principal. The school's other teachers were Mattie L. Boyd, Jennette Brown, and Ophelia Patterson. In the early 1920s, the original one-room schoolhouse was sold, and the county provided a larger, two-room, wood-frame building for the school. Shady Grove School closed in 1954 along with two other county schools for African Americans: Lucy and Newsum.

# CORDOVA GRAMMAR SCHOOL
## (ROSENWALD)

The Cordova School was one of the earliest schools for African American children in the area. The school's second building was constructed in 1923 with support from the Rosenwald Fund. The school was a single-story, wood-frame structure. According to the Commercial Appeal, Lethia Mahone was the school's teacher in 1907. In 1919, Mrs. L. Husbands was Cordova's principal, and Martha Woodruff and Ruth Jones were the school's other teachers. An article in the Memphis Press-Scimitar, Miss. Alma Roach was the school's principal in 1952. She had been at the school since 1928, and the school served approximately 119 children. The school's two other teachers were Miss Christine Mason and Miss Anna B. Coleman. According to the article, the school had a small kitchen but couldn't use it because it did not have running water, a refrigerator, or screened windows. In the late 1940's1940s, school cafeterias did not meet specific standards and could not serve hot meals. In 1944, the county installed lights inside the school. Cordova merged with the new Mt. Pisgah School in 1958.

# Chapter Six

# Schools in Southeast Shelby County (Collierville, East Memphis, Germantown, and Hickory Hill)

## COLLIERVILLE JR. HIGH SCHOOL (ROSENWALD)

One of the first schools in Collierville for African American children, Collierville Junior High School, was established around 1908. The school was sometimes called the Collierville-Byhalia School because of its location on Byhalia Road or the Collierville Rosenwald School. According to Shelby County Board minutes from 1908, Charles. W. Hurd was the principal of Collierville School. He remained the principal at least until 1909. In 1921, a new schoolhouse was built with the assistance of the Rosenwald Fund. In 1924, the teachers were members of the school's faculty: M.A. Sloan, Principal; Elizabeth Sloan, Priscilla Alexander, Annie Wilkes, Eva Alcorn, Minnie Bragg Williams, and Blanche Hurd.

In 1952, Odie L. Armour was serving as the school's principal. At that time, the school served grades 1 through 10 and enrolled 500 students. During this time, students used outdoor toilets, and an outdoor pump was used for water. In addition to Professor Armour, the following teachers were on the faculty during the 1952-1953 school year: Minnie Armour, Leroy Stovall, Booker T. Hayes, Daisy B. Scott, Lachree Ward Steverson, Irene Lane, Clementie Hughes, Lettie L. Poston, Harold Galloway, Lucille Wilson, Alma Holt, and E. Watson. From 1921 to the desegregation of schools at the end of the 1960s, Collierville School was the only junior high school for African Americans in Collierville.

Collierville Jr. High School closed in 1970, and the schoolhouse was converted into a single-family home. The home existed until it was torn down to make way for the new Nonconnah Parkway (Tennessee Route 385) going through Collierville. The property was eventually sold, and it remains vacant. The 1960s map image above shows Collierville Jr. High on Byhalia Road near Collierville Road circled. The early 2020 map image below shows the parcel of land that the school once stood on now in the shadow of Nonconnah Parkway.

Pictured left is Collierville-Byhalia School Principal Dr. Odie Lee Armour. He served as the principal of Collierville-Byhalia School from 1936 until his retirement in 1968. Professor Armour earned both a Bachelor of Science degree in 1929 and a Master of Science degree in Agricultural Education in 1952 from Tennessee A & I State College. After graduating from college, Dr. Armour was appointed to a teaching position at Geeter High School and taught briefly at Millington Jr. High before moving to Collierville. For 32 years, he and his wife, Minnie, proudly served Collierville's African American children and families. (Courtesy of the Tennessee State University Special Collection)

Pictured left is Collierville-Byhalia, teacher and wife of Dr. Armour, Minnie Greer Armour. Mrs. Armour earned both a Bachelor of Science degree in Home Economics in 1941 and a Master of Science degree in Secondary Education from Tennessee A & I State College in 1955. Mrs. Armour served as the school's vocational home economics teacher. She taught for 45 years in Shelby County, including 32 years at Collierville Junior High. One of her first teaching appointments was at Geeter High School. The O.L. and Minnie Greer Armour Science and Education Building on the campus of Lane College was named in honor of Mrs. Armour and her husband in 1985. (Courtesy of the Tennessee State University Special Collection)

# NESHOBA JUNIOR HIGH SCHOOL (ROSENWALD)

One of the first schools for African American children in the Neshoba Community was established in the late 1880s. In 1902, Neshoba School, then named the Germantown School, was a simple one-room schoolhouse that was located near present-day Southern Ave and Poplar Pike in the city of Germantown. According to the Commercial Appeal, N.P. Bradley and Gazella Watkins were teachers at the school from 1907 through 1909. In 1914, Mary A. Bradford was appointed the principal. During her nine-year tenure, a new five-room Rosenwald School was built in 1918. In addition to Principal Bradford, Mary Watkins, D. Hodges, and Jeanette Walker were teachers at the school in 1919. Nicholas Giles Watkins was named the principal in 1923. Shelby County Board records list the following teachers as part of the Neshoba faculty in 1924: Nicholas G. Watkins, principal; Pearl Lewis, Mary Watkins, Gazella Watkins Brown, Janie Hobson, Caroline Cato, Darthula Hodges, and Edna Griffin. The Neshoba School became a junior high school in 1926.

Significant improvements were made to the school buildings in 1952. The Shelby County School Board approved the addition of six rooms to the existing five rooms on campus. Additionally, a kitchen was added so students could have hot lunches. All welcomed the addition of indoor toilets, fountains, and an enlarged auditorium. Because of the increased space, eleventh grade was added that year. After 38 years as principal of Neshoba, Professor Watkins retired in 1961, and Mr. Joseph Simmons was appointed the new principal. In 1966, Professor Simmons was named principal of Capleville High School, and Professor Henry Grinner moved to Neshoba from the recently closed Bartlett Jr. High. As a result of desegregation efforts, the Neshoba Junior High School was closed in 1969. The building was lost to fire in 2001. (Courtesy of the Tennessee State University Special Collection)

Nicholas Giles Watkins, pictured left, served as the principal of Neshoba Junior High School from 1923 until his retirement in 1961. During his tenure as principal, the school transitioned from an elementary to a junior high. Professor Watkins was instrumental in getting a school bus to transport students to and from school. (Courtesy of the Tennessee State University Special Collection)

Pictured right is Principal Richard H. Neville. Professor Neville was a graduate of the LeMoyne Normal Institute. In addition to teaching in Germantown, he taught in Memphis, serving as a teacher at Carnes School before his appointment to principal of Greenwood School, Melrose High School, and Klondike Elementary. Principal Neville served as the principal of Melrose School during the transition from the original two-story, wood frame building to the new two-story brick building on Dallas Street in Orange Mound. (Courtesy of the Tennessee State University Special Collection)

# FOREST HILL GRAMMAR SCHOOL (ROSENWALD)

The Forest Hill School was established for African American children in Southeast Shelby County near present-day Germantown, TN, before 1907. According to Shelby County Board minutes, Etta Jones was the school's only teacher in 1907 and 1908. In 1909, Roxie Tucker Brown was documented as the principal, and Etta Jones served as the assistant. According to the Commercial Appeal, Lula Hodges and Manetha Jordan were teachers in 1919. In 1923, a new three-teacher Rosenwald school building was constructed on present-day Forest Hill-Irene Road in Germantown. According to 1924 school board records, Walter Mitchell was the principal, and Lutitia Saunders and Mary Fifer served as teachers. The school's faculty in 1952 consisted of Principal Mary Frances Perry and teachers Myrtle Greer Bell and Lila B. Anderson. The school consolidated with the nearby Neshoba Junior High School in 1957. Currently, the former school building is home to the Germantown Community Theatre. (Courtesy of a private collection)

Myrtle Greer Bell was a Forest Hill Grammar School teacher in the 1940s and 1950s. The sister of Minnie Greer Armour, Collierville Jr. High School Teacher, and wife of Collierville Jr. High Principal Dr. Odie L. Armour, Greer was a LeMoyne High School Department and Lane College graduate. During her career, she taught in the Shelby County School District for many years until her retirement in 1971. (Courtesy of the Murray State Digital Commons)

# HICKORY HILL GRAMMAR SCHOOL (ROSENWALD)

Hickory Hill Grammar School was located near the intersection of present-day Winchester and Hickory Hill Road. The school was first mentioned in the Commercial Appeal in 1897 when it was reported that the school near Germantown was burned. In 1907, Mrs. Gertrude Bradford was elected as the school's teacher. Records indicate that she served as the school's teacher until 1909. According to the Commercial Appeal, M. J. Clark and Lodia Robinson were teachers at Hickory Hill Grammar in 1919. In 1923, Hickory Hill School was one of ten schools in Shelby County to receive a new school building via the Rosenwald Fund. According to a 1952 article in the Memphis Press-Scimitar, the first school building was lost to fire, and the current building is the one that was erected in 1923. There was a kitchen, but it was only used when the county provided food. The kitchen had a stove and refrigerator provided by the community's parents. The school had outdoor water and toilets, and the indoor lights were provided by parents in 1948. In 1948, Florence Odessa Roberts Tate was elected the school's principal. She remained at Hickory Hill until being named assistant principal of Geeter High School in 1957, and Katie Coopwood was named principal. Miss Coopwood was a Fullview Grammar School teacher when she was appointed to Hickory Hill. Hickory Hill Grammar School closed in 1959.

Florence Odessa Roberts-Tate, pictured left, served as the principal of Hickory Hill Grammar School until 1957. Mrs. Roberts-Tate was born and raised in Germantown, TN. She was a 1945 graduate of LeMoyne College, earning a Bachelor of Science degree in Education, and a 1958 graduate of Tennessee A & I State College, earning a Master of Science degree in Educational Administration. In 1948, she was hired as a teacher at Cordova Grammar School. She was named assistant principal of Geeter High School in 1957 under the leadership of Dr. Joseph W. Falls. She served at Mt. Pisgah High and was named Shelby County supervisor in 1964. She retired as a guidance counselor at Germantown High School in 1984. She was a member of Delta Sigma Theta Sorority, Inc. (Courtesy of a private collection)

Katie F. Coopwood, pictured left, was appointed the principal of Hickory Hill in 1957. Miss Coopwood was a 1926 graduate of Manassas High School and a 1953 graduate of Lane College. Miss Coopwood was a teacher at Fullview School when she was named principal of Hickory Hill. Before her time at Hickory Hill, Principal Coopwood also served as a teacher at Bridgewater School. According to the Memphis Press-Scimitar, as a teacher at Bridgewater in 1952, she taught students in grades 3 through 5. At that time, she had taught at Bridgewater for eight years. (Courtesy of Lane College Archive)

# T. W. PATTERSON HIGH SCHOOL (ROSENWALD)

T. W. Patterson High School was located on Sanderlin Road and Mendenhall Road. The school was initially named the White Station School, the same as the school for white students located less than a mile away. The 1949 map image above shows the school bordered by Black Street to the south and Mendenhall Road to the east. That building was constructed in 1925. The small structure in front of Patterson School is the New Philadelphia Missionary Baptist Church. The present-day Mendenhall Commons Shopping Center and William Arnold Road nearby had yet to be developed at the time this photograph was taken. The school was mentioned for the first time in the Memphis Avalanche Newspaper in 1890. The article highlighted a visit to the school by the superintendent. The school's teacher was Turner W. Patterson. He is believed to be the school's first teacher. Professor Patterson is listed as the school's teacher in the 1907 and 1909 articles of the Commercial Appeal. Mr. Patterson died in 1918, and the Commercial Appeal named Professor Judge L. Clark, Sr. as the school's principal, with Emmie McNeil, Mary Bryant, and Beatrice White as the school's other teachers.

In 1924, Mrs. Bessie N. Jones was appointed Patterson's principal, and the following teachers made up the remainder of the faculty: Eliza Bridgeforth, Dora Harris, and Mrtyle Walker. In 1952, Mr. Chastene Thompson, who attended Patterson as a child, returned to teach at the school. The following year, he was named principal when Principal Bessie N. Jones retired. That same year, the school's name was officially changed to T.W. Patterson High School after Professor Turner W. Patterson. In 1961, Dr. William H. Sweet was named principal. He remained the school's principal until the school closed in 1966.

Bessie N. Jones, pictured left, was appointed the principal of T. W. Patterson School in 1924. While teaching in the White Station Community, she impacted the lives of thousands of children. She retired in 1953 after almost 30 years as principal of Patterson School. (Courtesy of the Murray State Digital Commons)

Chastene Thompson, pictured left, was appointed principal of Patterson High in 1953. Former Patterson principal, Bessie N. Jones, was one of his teachers when he attended Patterson for grades 1 through 8. Mr. Thompson was a 1943 Booker T. Washington High School and a 1950 graduate of Tennessee A & I State College graduate with a Bachelor of Science in History. He also earned a master's degree from Indiana State University. In 1962, he transferred to Porter Jr. High as assistant principal. Mr. Thompson was appointed the assistant principal of Klondike Elementary before being named principal of Peabody Elementary in 1973. (Courtesy of the Murray State Digital Commons)

# APPENDIX

# Rural Shelby County Schools and Their Elected Teachers in 1907

## First Civil District
**Friendship** – Sam Robinson, Musie Moseley
**Shady Grove** – Hattie Bolton
**Hays Grove** – Vivian Bolton
**Ludicia** – C.W. Harrison
**Home Ferry** – Thomas

## Second Civil District
**Millington** – John Payne
**Promised Land** – Jacob Crenshaw
**Upper Caanan** – Eliza B. Watson
**Bethlehem** – B. Threlkeld

## Third Civil District
**Lucy** – A.V. Coffee, P.G. Johnson
**Woodstock** – A.C. Boone, Flora Brown
**Remberton** – Anna Thomas
**Zion Hill** – Effie B. Vaucey
**Bolton Bottom** – T.U. Davis
**Noah's Chapel** – Sarah Dillard

## Fourth Civil District
**St. Mathews** – Bessie Thompson
**St. Paul** – Flora Maben
**Walsh** – Mattie Walker

## Seventeenth Civil District
**Benjestown** – Ada Horton, Hattie Huff
**Point** – Clara Blackwell
**Smoky Row** – Pinkie Thomas
**Island No. 40** – Mamie McPherson

## Second Commissioner's District
**Manassas** – Mrs. F.W. Semmes, Principal; Laura O. Johnson, Ella Mosely, Janetta Shivers
**New Chelsea** – Rose Washington

## Twelfth Civil District
**John's Chapel** – John Shaw, Callie Earthman
**Tip Top** – not elected

## Thirteenth Civil District
**Cow Street** – Simon P. Morris
**Brooks Avenue** – Simon P. Morris
**Geeter** – Lucy Jay
**Darwin** – Estelle Campbell
**Ensley** – John Looney
**Weaver** – Clara Blackwell

## Eleventh Civil District
**Germantown** – N.P. Bradley, Gazella Watkins
**Featherstone** – Hattie Watkins Alice Glady
**Hickory Hill** – Gertrude Bradford
**New Sardis** – W.J. Clark

## Fourteenth Civil District
**Menager Avenue** – J.W. Ribbons, Principal; Lula Brazelton, Addie Williams, and Matilda Bell
**President's Island** – Estelle Ware
**Elliston Avenue** – Sarah Black

## Sixteenth Civil District
**White Station** – T.W. Patterson
**Walnut Grove** – Alfred Clark and Lena B. Smith

## Eighteenth Civil District
**Melrose** – W.G. Foster, Laura Gwynn, and Mary Benton
**Scott Avenue** – Mary Fortson and Carrie Pinkston
**Greer's** – Hattie Gwynne
**Cane Creek** – Nicholson

## Eighth Civil District
**Arlington** – W.L. Cotter
**Brunswick** – Ella Granderson
**No. 12** – O.H. Gray
**Grays Creek** – Mary Taylor
**Pea Point** – Effie Hays

# Rural Shelby County Schools and Their Elected Teachers in 1907 (continued)

## Nineth Civil District
**Eads** – Luella Robinson
**Mt. Olive** – Willie Coleburn
**Mt. Pisgah** – T.F. Moore
**Morning Grove** – Sallie Gray
**Cordova** – Lethia Mahene
**Tan Yard** – Dan Seward

## Tenth Civil District
**St. James** – **Charlie Herd**
**Irene** – Jessie Campbell
**Forest Hill** – Etta Jones
**Shelby** – T.W. Cross

## Sixth Civil District
**Raleigh** – Cora P. Taylor
**Spring Hill** – Sallie Green
**Hogan's Chapel** – Katie Scruggs
**Leewood** – Mary Abbott
**Frayser** – Mattie Christopher
**Overton** – Hattie Huff

## Seventh Civil District
**Bartlett** – Rochelle Pinkston, Estella Knox
**Full View** – G.W. Thomas and Iola Yancey
**Bridgewater** – Alice Bernard
**Hill Chapel** – Susie Mosely
**Oak Grove** – Mary Homer
**Prosperity** – T.W. Johnson

(Source: Commercial Appeal – July 9, 1907)

# Rural Shelby County Schools and Their Elected Teachers in 1909

## First Civil District
**Ludicia** – Ollie Thomas
**Hays Grove** – Mertus S. Strong
**Home Ferry** – Sam Hill
**Mt. Sinai** – Vivian Bolton
**Shady Grove** – Hattie Bolton
**Friendship** – Ethel Bolton

## Second Civil District
**Millington** – William Jefferson, Principal; Flora Mebane, Assistant
**Upper Caanan** – Eliza Watson
**Williams Chapel** – Virginia Seward
**Promised Land** – John Hays
**Bethlehem** – Ada Boone

## Third Civil District
**Lucy** – A.C. Boone, Principal; Mary C. Bell, Assistant
**Woodstock** – Mattie Horton, Principal; Ella Perkins, Assistant
**Big Creek** – B. Threlkeld
**Noah's Chapel** – Geneva Threlkeld
**Rembert House** – Emma Haynes, Principal; Margaret Williams, Assistant

## Fourth Civil District
**Walsh** – Nina Fields
**St. Paul** – Bessie Thompson

## Seventeenth Civil District
**Benjestown** – Ada Horton, Principal; Hattie Huff, primary
**Point** – Jeanette Shivers
**Smoky Row** – Flora J. Brown

## Sixth Civil District
**Raleigh** – Katie Scruggs, Principal; Mattie Smith, Assistant
**Springhill** – Sallie Green
**Hogan's Chapel** – Mary Mitchell
**Leewood** – Mary Abbott
**Frayser** – Georgia Perry
**Overton** – Julia Osborne

## Seventh Civil District
**Bartlett** – Thomas W. Johnson, Principal
**Full View** – John Barnett, Principal; Osceola Alexander, Assistant
**Bridgewater** – Alice Bernard
**Hill Chapel** – Lucy Bailey, Principal; Easter Wade, Assistant
**Oak Grove** – Roschella Pinkston
**Prosperity** – G.W. Thomas, Sally Bentley

## Fifteenth Civil District
**Manassas** – Cora P. Taylor, Principal; Laura O. Johnson, Assistant; Ella Moseley, Assistant
**New Chelsea** – Mattie Richmond, Principal; Hattie Baker, Assistant

## Twelfth Civil District
**Jones Chapel** – Samuel W. Carnes
**Macdeonia** – Ethel Tuggle
**Payne** – Dicey Anderson

## Thirteenth Civil District
**Ensley** – J. H. Brown
**Geeter** – Callie Mathis, Estelle Campbell, Assistant
**Weaver** – Beulah Moss
**Menegar Avenue** – J. W. Ribbins, Principal; Lucy Jay, Estelle Ware
**President's Island** – Lula Brazelton, Principal; Elnora Franklin, Assistant

## Eleventh Civil District
**Germantown** – N. P. Bradley, Principal; Gazella Watkins, Assistant
**Featherstone** – Hattie Watkins, Principal; Eunice Roberts, Assistant
**Hickory Hill** – Gertrude Bradford
**New Sardis** – Jetson Clarke

# Rural Shelby County Schools and Their Elected Teachers in 1909 (continued)

## Sixteenth Civil District
**White Station** – Turner Patterson
**Kirby** – Amanda Threat
**Walnut Avenue** – Alfred Clarke

## Eighth Civil District
**Black's** – Obidiah Gray
**Arlington** – Alfred Clarke, Principal; Estelle Hegler, Assistant
**Brunswick** – Jerry Horne
**Gray's Creek** – Cecil Sales

## Nineth Civil District
**Eads** – Suvella Robinson
**Mt. Olive** – F. F. Moore
**Mt. Pisgah** – J. W. Hewlett
**Morning Grove** – Hattie Green
**Jones Chapel** – Eddie L. Cooper

## Eighteenth Civil District
**Melrose** – Mary Benton, Principal; Laura Gwin, Jessie Gwin, Levy D. Smith
**Scott Avenue** – Mary Fortson, Principal; Elizabeth Goldsby, Assistant
**Greer's** – Etta Danner

## Tenth Civil District
**Collierville** – Charlie Hurd
**Fleming Grove** – Martha Bragg
**McKinney** – Jessie Campbell
**Shelby** – Milus J. Clarke
**Forest Hill** – Roxie Tucker, Principal; Etta Jones, Assistant

(Source: Commercial Appeal – July 25, 1909)

# Rural Shelby County Schools and Their Elected Teachers in 1919

## First District

**St. Paul** – I.N. Jackson and Gladys Harper

**St. Matthews** – Jennie Belle Horn and May Bolden

**Smoky Row** – Sidney Palmer and Hazel Thompson

**Benjestown** – Lillie Williams, Ethel Wells, and Irma Poston

**Promised Land** – Sarah White

**Walsh** – S. Palmer and M. Warren

**Upper Caanan** – C.H. Dixon and Annie Hughes

**Bethlehem** – W.L. Trotter and Annie Stout

**Millington** – Henry L. Peterson, Hattie Dandridge, Emma Randolph, and Pearl Young

**Lucy** – Jacob Currin, Beatrice Willis, and Lucy Thomas

**Shelby County Training School (Woodstock)** – T.J. Johnson, Principal; J. Gertrude Johnson, girls' industries; F.E. Cleaves, general science and hygiene; E.J. Ford, reading and spelling; E.M. Bridges, millinery and handicraft; E.Y. Osby head teacher, English; E. Mitchell, music and primary; F.A. Lane, matron and domestic science; A.R. Davis, primary; J.B. Horn, laundering; L.J. Williams, broom making, carpentry; J.A. Oliver, vocational agriculture; F.A. Darrel, mathematics

**Gilfield** – S.A. Robinson and Orelia Strong

**Williams Chapel** – Minnie MacElwee and Esther Adams

**Noah's Chapel** – Beulah Robinson and L.M. Herring

**Bolton Bottom** – Ethel Woodward, Hattie Threlkeld, and Willie Hunt

**Shady Grove** – Eupheuma Hall

**Hays Grove** – Vivian Bolton, Geneva Threlkeld, Cleo Bolton, Rowena Johnson

**Friendship** – Essie Gibes

**Ludicia** – Cora Crafford, Dora Belle Braden

**Home Ferry** – C.E. Stewart, Helen Albright

**Mt. Sinai** – Mattie Shaw and Helen Shaw

## Second District

**Frayser** – Matilda Bell and Serena Anderson

**Overton Crossing (Dickens)** – Daisy Stevens and Mamie Warren

**Hogan's Chapel** – Geneva Fulton

**Manassas** – Cora P, Taylor, Principal; Myrtle Lewis, Rubye Berry, Carrie Pinkston, Emma Johnston, Katie Scruggs, Esther Doggett, Susie Davis, Roxie Brown, Florence Phillips, Audrey Johnson, Isabelle Greenleaf, Amanda Woodfin, Beulah Moss, and Sylvia Owens

**New Chelsea** – Hattie Baker and Virginia Johnson

**Leewood** – Lillie Pierce and M. Barnes

**Spring Hill** – Zavan Felton, Carrie Johnson, Felicia Harris, and Mattie Boyd

**Prosperity** – Reda Johnson and Roxie Becton

**Bartlett** – Malinda Simpson, Grace Johnson, and Lassie McCully

**Full View** – Edmonia Taylor, Alice Harper, and Audrey Nelson

**Oak Grove** – Ada Mullins and Fannie Porter

**Bridgewater** – Josephine Simpson, Susie Smith, and Jennie V. McCulley

**Hollywood** – Helen Pointer and M. Ross

**Hyde Park** – Amelia Dandridge

# Rural Shelby County Schools and Their Elected Teachers in 1919 (continued)

## Third District

**Weaver:** Simon P. Morris, Sarah Morris, Ophelia Ford, and Lena Wortch

**White's Chapel:** Ada Stafford

**Coahoma Landing:** Susie Peoples

**Geeter:** Louise Polk and Annie Perkins

**Ensley:** J.H. Brown

**Brooks Avenue:** May McNicholas and Ida Ford

**Hamner-Taylor:** Reggie Bryant, Callie Earthman, Edna Plunkett and Sherwood Rutherford

**Oakville:** Devonia Matthews and Helen D. Casey

**Payne:** Ruth Clark

**Jones Chapel:** Mattie Robinson

**Capleville:** Lutitia Tyus, Lula Jones, and Pearl Tillman

**Florida Street:** M.E. Currin, Mattie Lynk, Addie Tanlery, Maggie Radcliff, Viola Overton, Estelle Campbell, Callie Mathis, Mabel Crump, Sallie Cummings, and Etta Drake

**Morning View:** Myrtle Jones and Marie Rodgers

**President's Island:** Elnora Howard and Lula Crawford

**Greer's:** Julia Adams and Lizzie M. Hunt

**St. Stephens:** Elise Edgington

**Scott Avenue:** Mattie Smith, Mattie Cash, M. Johnson, Julia Peterson, Ophelia Hunt, Beatrice Moore, Juanita Peterson, Eliza Cotton, and Erwina Jones

**Magnolia:** M. Taylor

**Mt. Zion:** Blanche Forman

**Shelby:** C.W. Herd and Sammie Wilson

**Fleming Grove:** Lillian Jordan and Priscilla True

**Melrose:** R.H. Fleming, Mattie Nelson, Blanche Martin, G. Adams, Frances Reems, U. P. Edison, Levy Smith, Mary Stokes, Florence Banks, A.B. O'Neil, and Bessie Wilson

**Cane Creek:** D. Anderson and E. Nicholson

**White Station:** J.L. Clark, Emmie McNeil, Mary Bryant and Beatrice White

**Neshoba:** Mary Bradford, Mary Watkins, D. Hodges, and Jeanette Walker

**Hickory Hill:** M.J. Clark and Lodia Robinson

**Prospect:** Anna Tuggle and Alice Harper

**Sardis:** Hattie Bradley and Alice Dean

**Oak Hill:** Zolania Taylor, Esther Fields, and Odelia Olds

**Arlington:** Cecil Sales, Annie Hays, Mattie Harris, and Ida Branch

**Wells:** Estella Haglar and Omega Hays

**Blacks:** Sallie G. Belot and Rochester Fairly

**Bush Grove:** Ira Emery, Maggie Buckley, and Martha Hayes

**Morning Grove:** Annie Phillips and Bessie Rice

**Eads:** E.A. Teague, Ora Teague, W.C. Tyus, and L.R. Tyus

**Mt. Pisgah:** Fannie Beason, A.L. Davis, and Nora Grey

**Jones Chapel:** - A.J. Edwards and Willie M. Thompson

**Price:** Lena Thomas

**Mt. Olive:** Nicholas Watkins and Emma Franklin

**Tan yard:** M. Frayser

**Forest Hill:** Lula Hodges and Manetha Jordan

**Wright's Chapel:** Alma Hobson

**St. Paul:** E. Bridgeport

**St. Mark:** Susie Truehart and A. Herd

**McKinney:** Florence Fields

# Rural Shelby County Schools and Their Elected Teachers in 1924

**Arlington**: Cecil Sales, Principal; Ida Branch, Lucile Slack, Rowena Dandridge, and Virgie Hayes

**Bartlett**: Clara Prince, Principal; Justine Broglin, Helen Albright, Octavia Nelson, Emma Price, and Bessie Nichols

**Bailey**: Media White, Principal

**Benjestown**: M. H. Moreland, Principal; Ethel McQueen, Ellarine Tisdale, Clara Boyd, and Lucy Horton

**Bethlehem**: Lucy Thomas, Principal; Hattie Stewart and Victor Williams

**Blacks**: Elvira Stuart, Principal

**Bolton Bottom** – J.E. Taylor, Principal; Lizzie Taylor

**Brunswick**: W.I. Trotter, Principal; Sallie Belote, Susie Martin, Shellie Martin, Ora Hammond, and Theresa Horton

**Bridgewater**: Georgia Tyus Sylver, Principal; Pearl Chatman, Rosa Ford, Lucy Clemons Newbern, and Alma Roach

**Brooks Avenue**: Ida Ford, Principal; Ethel Sarah Morris and Dora Whitworth

**Coahoma Landing**: J.W. Cross, Principal

**Hamner-Taylor**: Callie Earthman, Principal; Mattie Robinson, Effie Washington, Theodore Robinson, and Ada Henderson

**Hays Grove**: Edward Gray, Principal; Ezzia Woods, Allie Ruth Davis, and Constance Bolton

**Hickory Hill**: M.J. Clark, Principal; Alberta Bragg, Alice Brown, and Thelma Morris

**Home Ferry**: Estella Heglar, Principal; Dora Braden

**Hogan's Chapel**: Deanie Mae Banks, Principal; Pearl Banks

**Island Forty**: T.M. Mitchell, Principal

**Jones Chapel**: N. Garth, Principal; Maggie Edwards

**Ludicia**: William Franklin, Principal; Evalina Franklin

**Lucy**: Minnie Williams, Principal; Tillie Mullens

**Log Union**: Ira Emery, Principal; Millie Reeder, Bessie Westbrook

**Morning Grove**: Iola Gardner, Principal; Lillian Cox and Sarah Pinkston

**McKinney**: Irene Raiford, Principal; Celia Stansbury

**Mount Olive**: Lucile Hawthorne, Principal; Addie Stafford

**Promised Land**: Willie Sanderlin, Principal

**Prosperity**: Narcissa Hart, Principal; Armenia Franklin and Jennie Breathett

**Pierce Chapel**: Carrie Newsom, Principal

**Rembert Springs**: Rosa Nelson, Principal; Macie Bates

**Shady Grove**: C.E. Stewart, Principal; Mattie L. Boyd, Jennette Brown, and Ophelia Patterson

**Shelby**: Mary Martin, Principal; M. Winbush

**Shiloh**: Maggie Smith, Principal

**Smoky Row**: Beatrice McGuire, Principal

**St. Paul**: Cora Lee Taylor, Principal

**St. Stephens**: Josephine Williamson, Principal; Geneva Baker

**Spring Hill**: Zavan Felton, Principal; Luvenia Felton, Lossie Meadows, Felicia Owens, and Lillian McClarine

**St. Mathews**: I. N. Jackson, Principal; Inesta Wells and Rosa Bowden

**Tan Yard**: T.U. Davis, Principal

**Capleville**: Jacob Currin, Principal; Nannie Little, Mary Allen, Leathy Kohlheim, and Samella Miller

**Jerusalem**: Sallie C. Lott, Principal

# Rural Shelby County Schools and Their Elected Teachers in 1924 (continued)

**Collierville**: M.A. Sloan, Principal,; Elizabeth Sloan, Priscilla Alexander, Annie Wilkes, Eva Alcorn, Minnie Bragg Williams, and Blanche Hurd

**Cordova**: Lizzie Husbands, Principal; Martha Woodruff and Ruth Jones

**Ensley**: Phillip Brooks, Principal

**Eads**: E.A. Teague, Principal; Ora Teague, Alice Wherry, Viola Flowers, Minnie Lee Kennedy, Lou Berta Reid, and Ora Montgomery

**Forest Hill**: Walter Mitchell, Principal; Lutitia Saunders and Mary Fifer

**Frayser**: Serena Anderson, Principal; Matilda Bell

**Friendship**: Essie Banks, Principal

**Full View**: O.H. Gray, Principal; Marquerite Hunt Ewing, Willie M. Hawkins, and Ethel Gray

**Geeter**: Joseph W. Falls, Principal; Montee Falls, Queen Lamar, Vernita Grigsby, Geraldine Simms, Sammie E. Wilson, Ophelia Ford, and Jessie Hilliard

**Gilfield**: Mattie Smith, Principal; Bessie Robinson

**Mt. Pisgah**: W.C. Tyus, Principal; Laura Tyus, Eliza Anderson, Catherine Twine, and Ary Bailey

**Millington**: Luckie C. Sharp, Principal; Gladys Sharp, Rubye White, Pearlina Bartlett, A.T. Williams, Scottie Purdy, Sara Stams, Leatha Hardy, and L.J. Williams

**Mt. Sinai**: Nora Stewart, Principal; Bessie Shaw

**Mt. Zion**: Blanche Foreman, Principal

**New Sardis**: Hattie Bradley, Principal; Lucy Dandridge and Elnora Harper

**Newsum**: Ernestine Johnson, Principal; Alice Waters

**Neshoba**: Nicholas G. Watkins, Principal; Pearl Lewis, Mary Watkins, Gazella Watkins Brown, Janie Hobson, Caroline Cato, Darthula Hodges, and Edna Griffin

**Noah's Chapel**: Dovie Gleaves, Principal; Henrietta Becton

**Oak Grove**: Ada Mullens, Principal; Maggie B. Frazier, Minnie L. Becton, and Mary Greenlaw

**Oakville**: Nellie Foster, Principal; Bernadine Morris

**Overton Crossing**: Lillie Dickerson, Principal; Leathy Moss

**Walsh**: Darthula Dawkins, Principal; Nina B. Allen

**Wells**: Mattie McNeace, Principal; Callie Ingram

**Weaver**: Minnie Toliver, Principal; Willie Belle Cooper, Mary Peete, Iola Thompson, and Ludorn Saddler

**White's Chapel**: Suvella Benton, Principal; Myrtle Belle

**White Station**: Bessie Jones, Principal; Eliza Bridgeforth, Dora Harris, and Myrtle Walker

**Williams' Chapel**: George Spicer, Principal; Blanche Currie

**Zion Hill**: Mattie Geeter, Principal; Allura Galloway

(Source: Commercial Appeal – November 17, 1924)

# The Rosenwald Schools in Shelby County Schools

1. Arlington School
2. Augusta Rosenwald School
3. Bartlett School
4. Barret's Chapel School
5. Benjestown School
6. Black's School
7. Bolton Bottom School
8. Bridgewater School
9. Brooks Avenue School
10. Brunswick School
11. Collierville School
12. Cordova School
13. Eads School (St. Matthews No. 1)
14. Ellendale School
15. Forest Hill School
16. Geeter School
17. Gilfield School
18. Hamner-Taylor School
19. Hayes Grove School
20. Hickory Hill School
21. Home Ferry School
22. Leewood School
23. Log Union School
24. Lucidia School
25. Ludicia School
26. Lucy School
27. Macedonia School
28. Magnolia School
29. Manassas School
30. Melrose School
31. Millington School
32. Mt. Sinai School
33. Neshoba School
34. Noah's Chapel School
35. Oak Grove School
36. Oak Hill School
37. Oakville School
38. Overton School
39. Park Ave. School
40. Pisgah School
41. Price's Chapel School
42. Prosperity School
43. Rembert Springs School
44. Rosenwald School
45. St. Matthew School
46. St. Paul School
47. Sardis-McKinney School
48. Shady Grove School
49. Shelby-Bailey School
50. South Memphis School
51. Spring Hill School
52. Walsh School
53. Weaver School
54. Wells School
55. White's Chapel School
56. White Station School (Patterson)
57. Williams Chapel
58. Williams School
59. Woodstock School

(Source: Commercial Appeal – October 2, 2003; Compiled by Fisk University)

# About the Author:

# Wynn E. Earle, Jr. Ed.D.

Dr. Wynn Earle, Jr. is a native Memphian currently employed by the Memphis Shelby County School District as principal of Kingsbury Elementary School. He graduated from Overton High School, the University of Memphis, and Union University, where he earned his Doctor of Education Degree in Instructional Leadership. In 2022, Earle authored the book *Early African American Schools in Memphis.* He is an avid reader of most things Memphis and a collector of vintage and rare books, photographs, and ephemera documenting academic life for African Americans locally and nationally.